D0930428

Letters to Margaret Bridges
(1915–1919)

John Masefield

Letters to Margaret Bridges (1915–1919)

edited by

DONALD STANFORD

CARCANET

in association with MidNAG

First published in Great Britain 1984
by the Carcanet Press
208 Corn Exchange Building, Manchester M4 3BQ
in association with Mid Northumberland Arts Group
Town Hall, Ashington, Northumberland
© 1984 John Masefield's letters and poems:
       The Literary Estate of John Masefield
© 1984 Margaret Bridges' letters:
       The Lord Bridges
© 1984 Introduction and Notes:
       Donald E. Stanford
Armistice © 1984 Carcanet Press Ltd

Masefield, John
  Letters to Margaret Bridges (1915–1919).
  1. Masefield, John—Biography   2. Poets,
  English—20th century—Biography
  I. Title   II. Stanford, Donald
  821'.912   PR6025.A77Z/

ISBN 0 85635 477 5/ISBN 0 904790 37 1

The Publishers acknowledge financial assistance
from the Arts Council of Great Britain

Typesetting by Paragon Photoset, Aylesbury
Printed in Great Britain by
Short Run Press Ltd, Exeter

Contents

Introduction 7
August, 1914 13

1915

1,	2	*June*	From Margaret Bridges	17
	3	*June*	From John Masefield	18
	4	*July*	From Margaret Bridges	19
		Lollingdon Downs		20

1917

5,	6	*January, February*	From John Masefield	22
	7	*March*	From Margaret Bridges	24
	8	*March*	From John Masefield	25
	9	*March*	From Margaret Bridges	26
10–14		*March*	From John Masefield	27
		Sonnets		32
15–23		*April*	From John Masefield	33
	24	*April*	From Margaret Bridges	43
25–27		*April, May*	From John Masefield	44
		The Downland		48
28–44		*May–October*	From John Masefield	49
		The Blacksmith		70
45–51		*November*	From John Masefield	73

Letters from America, 1918

52–61 *January–April*   81
       We Danced   93
62–71 *April–June*   94
       Armistice, by Elizabeth Daryush   107

1919

72–73 *January*   From John Masefield   108

       Notes   112
       Acknowledgements   123

Illustrations

Margaret Bridges   frontispiece
John Masefield in uniform
Edward (later Lord Bridges)   25
   Margaret's brother
Wheeled stretchers taking the wounded   39
   from the firing line
American ambulance on shell-swept road   45
   near Verdun
Margaret Bridges   65
Elizabeth Daryush   106
   Margaret's sister

For Maryanna

Introduction

These hitherto unpublished letters of the poet John Masefield (1878–1967) to Margaret Bridges, daughter of the poet Robert Bridges, were written between 1915 and 1919 during the tensions and suffering of World War I. War and its effect on the home front in England, and later, in America, and also its effect on Anglo-American relations, are major themes of the correspondence; but Masefield also discusses matters of general literary and cultural interest as well as his response to the American social scene during his two trips to the United States.

At the time his letters to Margaret Bridges begin (27 June 1915) John Masefield had become famous as the author of *Salt-Water Ballads* (1902) and of the narrative poems *The Everlasting Mercy* (1911) and *The Widow in the Bye Street* (1912). At the outbreak of war he and his family were dividing their time between 13 Well Walk in Hampstead and their country home, Lollingdon, an old farmhouse near Wallingford, in the Thames Valley and on the edge of the Berkshire Downs. In the spring of 1917 the family — Masefield's wife Constance (referred to in the letters as Con) and the two children, Judith aged thirteen and Lewis almost seven — moved to Hill Crest on Boar's Hill, Oxford, where they were neighbours of the Bridges family — Robert Bridges (1844–1930), his wife, their daughters Margaret and Elizabeth, and their son Edward — all of whom are referred to in the letters. At this time Bridges had been Poet Laureate for almost four years. Masefield was to succeed him as Poet Laureate in 1930.

Masefield's affection and admiration for Margaret Bridges, eleven years his junior, are evident in every letter, an affection which was shared by Masefield's family. Mrs Masefield wrote of her in her diary for 18 January 1915: 'Margaret Bridges walked over from Yattendon. She is so straight and strong and clever. I like her more than any girl I know.'* She was born in London on 10 October 1889, the second daughter of Robert Bridges. She grew up in the village of Yattendon, Berkshire, where the Bridges family had been living since 1884. Her mother, Monica, was the daughter of the architect Alfred Waterhouse. In 1907 she and her family moved to Chilswell, a house designed by Robert Bridges himself, on Boar's Hill, overlooking the city of Oxford. Margaret developed her talent for music and played the violin. From the autumn of 1915 (perhaps earlier) until late April 1917 she made her contribution to the war effort by cooking at a convalescent camp in the Boulogne area. In the summer of 1917 she was studying forestry, and by August she was 'foresting', as her father put it, in Wales where she stayed until the summer or autumn of 1918. Shortly after the war she became engaged to Horace Joseph, Senior Philosophical Tutor at New College, Oxford. They were married on 3 July 1919. She died of tuberculosis on 25 April 1926. A few weeks after her death, on the urging of his wife, who hoped to keep him from brooding over the loss of his daughter, her father set to work on *The Testament of Beauty* (1929).

Of the sixty-seven letters from Masefield in this volume all except the last two were written during the period of World War I when he was supporting England's war effort. He saw at first hand the battlefields of Gallipoli; he visited the battlefield of the Somme a number of times; he went twice to the United States in the years 1914–18. According to letter 32, when the war broke out in the summer of 1914 Masefield was at a lodge in Ireland where he met Margaret for the first time. In February he accepted work with the Red Cross at the British Red Cross Hospital for French wounded at Arc-en-Barrois, a village near Chaumont, in Haute Marne, about sixty miles from the front. He spent six weeks there as an orderly, billeted at the Lion d'Or, returning to England in early April. He then began his attempt to raise money for an open-air field hospital in the Vosges, a project which eventually had to be abandoned. On 27 June 1915 he wrote his first letter in this volume to Margaret. In mid-July 1915 he made his second trip to war-torn France where for two weeks he visited hospitals in the Tours area to gather information for setting up field hospitals in the Vosges.

At the end of July Masefield was invited to take charge of an expedition to reinforce the motor-boat ambulance service which carried English and French wounded from the battle areas of Gallipoli to the Allies' base at Mudros Bay, on the island of Lemnos sixty miles distant. He arrived in the Gallipoli area in September, too late to witness the major battles of 25 April at

Cape Hellas and Anzac and of 6 August at Suvla. He developed dysentery and returned to England in mid-October. He was soon at work preparing for a lecture tour in America, sponsored by the J.B. Pond Lyceum Bureau of New York City. Though mainly on literary subjects, the lectures were designed to increase interest in England and in the war aims of the Allies, at a time when America was neutral. This, his first American tour, lasted from early January to the middle of March 1916. (Incidentally, this was not Masefield's first visit to America: as a boy he had spent two years in and near New York City.) On his return to England he began writing his book *Gallipoli*, which was published in September 1916. It is an eloquent account of the courage and suffering of the British, Australian, and New Zealand troops during a campaign that ended in failure. Masefield's detailed description of the terrain, which he had personally examined, lends authenticity to his description of the battles. The book, which went through several editions, was a success in England, and especially in America where it strengthened sympathy for the Allies' cause.

Masefield undertook a third trip to France, from the end of August to the end of October 1916, to collect material for a report to the American press on America's contribution to the war. He visited the Verdun area and made a brief inspection of the battlefield of the Somme. He was commissioned by Field Marshal Sir Douglas Haig to write a chronicle of the battle. Back in England, he wrote his second letter to Margaret on 18 January 1917, and by the time he wrote his third letter, 26 February 1917, he had returned to France for his fourth visit which was to last until June. He made frequent and extensive inspections of the Somme, learning the terrain by heart for his two books, *The Old Front Line* (1917) and *The Battle of the Somme* (1919). The first is a detailed description of the front line in the British sector as it existed on 1 July 1916, at the time of the big attack. The second describes the battle which lasted from 1 July to 18 November. The Allies conquered 125 square miles of territory. The British lost 400,000 men, the French 200,000.

In April 1917 Masefield's wife moved the family into Hill Crest, where he joined them on his return from France in June. He set to work on the preface of his book on the Battle of the Somme. He was not permitted access to the Brigade and Battalion diaries and other records, so his preface had to become a book entitled *The*

Old Front Line, published in December 1917, in an edition of 20,000 copies.

In November the Pond Lyceum Bureau organized another American tour for Masefield, which was to last four months. He arrived in New York in January 1918 to begin his extensive round of lecture engagements, which took him to the West Coast as well as to the Middle-West and to several of the eastern and southern states. When his original schedule was completed in April, the YMCA arranged for Masefield to give a series of impromptu talks in army camps of the West and the South, which he completed in August. America was now at war with Germany and Masefield was enthusiastically welcomed as a friend and ally. Letters 52–71 contain his responses to the American scene.

Masefield was very much aware of the difficulties that had arisen between America and England from the Revolution of 1775 on, and he refers to them in several of his letters, especially in number 39. It was his mission to foster goodwill between the two countries, to ascertain the attitude of America towards the war and report back to his superiors. There was considerable isolationism in America prior to its entry into the war in April 1917. Yet America's response to the Masefield mission was positive. An article in the *Literary Digest*, 5 February 1916, entitled 'Masefield again in America', calls him England's greatest living poet, and refers to his stay in America as a young man in 1895–7, when he did various odd jobs including work in a carpet factory and acting as handy boy in a Sixth Avenue saloon. A cartoon memorializes his visit to this same saloon in 1916. In May 1917, a few weeks after America's declaration of war on Germany, Masefield published an article in *Harper's Monthly Magazine*, entitled 'The Harvest of the Night', describing the work of the American Ambulance Field Service in France. An editorial introduction summarizes Masefield's own work as a member of the Red Cross in France.

In his letters to Margaret, Masefield describes the America of the war years with a poet's observant eye and sensibility. In letter 61, from Seattle, for example, he writes eloquently of his view from the hotel at Puget Sound which is full of sailing and steam ships, and in the next letter he is enthusiastic about the beauties of the forests of Oregon in spring. By the time we reach letter 66 we are in what Masefield calls 'the real South', a section of America which especially appealed to his sense of history.

The last two letters, written a few weeks after the Armistice, are concerned with Margaret's impending marriage to Horace Joseph. Margaret Bridges carefully preserved all these letters from her friend and mentor. They were found among the Bridges Papers collected by her brother Edward, the first Lord Bridges. In 1978 the letters were deposited, with other Bridges Papers, in the Bodleian Library, Oxford, by the second Lord Bridges.

I have included a few letters of this period from Margaret Bridges to Masefield. They were recently discovered at the Humanities Research Center, University of Texas.

Included in this volume also are a number of poems by Masefield which were written about the same time he was carrying on his correspondence with Margaret Bridges. During the years 1914–18 Masefield, who as we have seen, was heavily engaged in war-related work and in the writing of several books in prose about the conflict, seldom dealt with the war in his poetry. *Sonnets* (containing sixty-one sonnets) was published in 1916 and was several times reprinted. The chief subject is Beauty wherever it is found, but especially as it is found in nature. There are very few topical references. *Lollingdon Downs* (1917) celebrates the beauty and tranquillity of the Thames Valley near Wallingford where Masefield and his family settled just before the war, in an old house which they named Lollingdon Farm.

Masefield had not been adverse to depicting scenes of violence and horror in his verse, as in *The Everlasting Mercy* and *The Widow in the Bye Street*, but during the period he was writing to Margaret he evidently composed poetry as a means of escape from the turmoil of the times. And, it may be noted, immediately after the war he wrote one of his most cheerful optimistic narrative poems, the Chaucerian *Reynard the Fox*.

But there were exceptions. 'August, 1914' is a moving address to the English, composed immediately after England had declared war on Germany. Beginning with stanzas praising the quiet and charm of the Thames Valley, he continues with a meditation on the conflicts of the past when so many Englishmen left their farms and families to die on foreign battlefields, and he concludes with the realization that it all must happen again. During a public appearance in 1916 at Yale University, he broke down during the reading of this poem when he reached the line 'And died (uncouthly most) in foreign land', and for a moment he could not continue. He asked to be excused for not finishing the verses, and went on to read another of his poems. The sonnet 'Here where we stood together . . .' refers to the Gallipoli campaign. Skyros and Seddul Bahr are mentioned. Skyros, the island on which Rupert Brooke died and was buried, was a naval base during the fighting. Seddul Bahr was the scene of one of the most disastrous battles of the campaign. The British and Australian soldiers were buried where they fell. The succeeding sonnet, 'I saw her like a shadow . . .' probably refers to Gallipoli, and 'Time being an instant . . .' is a lament for the dead of all wars. Several of the poems selected from *Lollingdon Downs* refer to death in battle although the war is not their primary subject. The vigorous poem 'The Blacksmith' was written in 1916 during Masefield's first visit to the United States. The sombre 'The Downland' is included as an example of Masefield's sensitive and varied response to the Downs. His love for them was also shared by Margaret Bridges.

I have rounded off the poems in this volume with 'Armistice' written by Margaret Bridges' sister, the distinguished poet Elizabeth Daryush. The manuscript of the poem was found in her desk after her death in April 1977. It was probably written on or shortly after 11 November 1918, but it was not published in her lifetime.

DONALD E. STANFORD

August, 1914

How still this quiet cornfield is to-night!
By an intenser glow the evening falls,
Bringing, not darkness, but a deeper light;
Among the stooks a partridge covey calls.

The windows glitter on the distant hill;
Beyond the hedge the sheep-bells in the fold
Stumble on sudden music and are still;
The forlorn pinewoods droop above the wold.

An endless quiet valley reaches out
Past the blue hills into the evening sky;
Over the stubble, cawing goes a rout
Of rooks from harvest, flagging as they fly.

So beautiful it is, I never saw
So great a beauty on these English fields,
Touched by the twilight's coming into awe,
Ripe to the soul and rich with summer's yields

*   *   *

These homes, this valley spread below me here,
The rooks, the tilted stacks, the beasts in pen,
Have been the heartfelt things, past-speaking dear
To unknown generations of dead men,

Who, century after century, held these farms,
And, looking out to watch the changing sky,
Heard, as we hear, the rumours and alarms
Of war at hand and danger pressing nigh.

And knew, as we know, that the message meant
The breaking off of ties, the loss of friends,
Death, like a miser getting in his rent,
And no new stones laid where the trackway ends.

The harvest not yet won, the empty bin,
The friendly horses taken from the stalls,

The fallow on the hill not yet brought in,
The cracks unplastered in the leaking walls.

Yet heard the news, and went discouraged home,
And brooded by the fire with heavy mind,
With such dumb loving of the Berkshire loam
As breaks the dumb hearts of the English kind,

Then sadly rose and left the well-loved Downs,
And so by ship to sea, and knew no more
The fields of home, the byres, the market towns,
Nor the dear outline of the English shore,

But knew the misery of the soaking trench,
The freezing in the rigging, the despair
In the revolting second of the wrench
When the blind soul is flung upon the air,

And died (uncouthly, most) in foreign lands
For some idea but dimly understood
Of an English city never built by hands
Which love of England prompted and made good.

       *   *   *

If there be any life beyond the grave,
It must be near the men and things we love,
Some power of quick suggestion how to save,
Touching the living soul as from above.

An influence from the Earth from those dead hearts
So passionate once, so deep, so truly kind,
That in the living child the spirit starts,
Feeling companioned still, not left behind.

Surely above these fields a spirit broods,
A sense of many watchers muttering near
Of the lone Downland with the forlorn woods
Loved to the death, inestimably dear.

A muttering from beyond the veils of Death
From long-dead men, to whom this quiet scene

Came among blinding tears with the last breath,
The dying soldier's vision of his queen.

All the unspoken worship of those lives
Spent in forgotten wars at other calls
Glimmers upon these fields where evening drives
Beauty like breath, so gently darkness falls.

Darkness that makes the meadows holier still,
The elm-trees sadden in the hedge, a sigh
Moves in the beech-clump on the haunted hill,
The rising planets deepen in the sky.

And silence broods like spirit on the brae,
A glimmering moon begins, the moonlight runs
Over the grasses of the ancient way
Rutted this morning by the passing guns.

1 *1 June*   *76 Rue Beaureprive, Boulogne*

Dear Mr Masefield, Thank you so much for your letter and your most kind offer to me to come and join your Hospital. I should like it above all things. I think you know that my experience of actual nursing is small, but of course I should be very glad to turn my hand to anything that I can do — cooking or music. I do hope that you will be able to get everything satisfactorily settled.

I am comfortably settled here, and hard at work — Office work from 10 to 6, writing and answering enquiries, and plenty of concerts at the different camps in the evenings — violin-playing, and playing endless accompaniments. The Concerts are a great joy, and I imagined that I was quite contented with the Office work until your letter came this morning, and then I realised how much better I should like the other sort of work. I have never done so much sitting still and writing before.

It is so very good of you to have thought of me. I expect you have settled on all your staff. If you did happen to be looking out for any probationers or general workers there is a girl (about 30) with me here, a Miss Hamersley, who has lived a lot in the colonies and is used to all sorts of manual work cooking etc and once had some hospital training. She is at present doing canteen work and has been here for 6 months. She would like to do some nursing, and she is the right sort — thoroughly sensible — and practical. I only mention her in case you are wanting that sort of person.

I shall not say anything about leaving my Office to the head, Sir Huchewn Poë, until I hear more definitely from you. He took some trouble to get me over here, and may not like my leaving. If you are not coming over until July, I *might* go home for a few days and come out with you and the rest. I have none of the right sort of clothes here and should have to think about getting those.

I'm writing to tell them at home of your offer. I don't think they will have any objections — but it is possible that they may, and I don't know whether you will perhaps have said anything to Father or Mother when you last saw them.

Thank you so very much. It is lovely to think that I may join you in a few weeks, and I am most grateful to you for thinking of me, and I shall anxiously await further news.

Forgive this badly-written letter, written rather late at night. I write better than this in the office.

I am so glad to think Mrs Masefield is coming out. Please give her my love. Yours very sincerely   *Margaret Bridges*

2   *24 June*   *Boulogne*

Dear Mr Masefield, I was prepared for the contents of your letter by hearing from Mother that the French insisted on very considerable modifications of your scheme and that you had applied to the Italian Gov't. I am so very sorry that there is this further delay. I was told by a Nurse who talked with some authority that the Italians were refusing outside help, and were well equipped with Hospitals. I hope if this is the case that they will write and tell you at once so as to save further waiting, which must be most irksome to you, and that you will then be able to pursue the Argonne scheme.

I am going on here with the same work at present. I have thought of signing on for 6 months and going into a military Hospital here if your scheme quite falls thro'. Miss H. will probably be given the management of a new canteen that will be started soon for a new camp, and I might have joined her and run the music of that. But I'm very uncertain, and so anxious to join you that I shall try not to commit myself to anything definite until I hear from you. No time for more.

I hope you are all well. I would like an afternoon on the downs. I read the Synge book in a hayfield on Sunday morning and much enjoyed it. Yours very sincerely   *Margaret Bridges*

3   *27 June*   *Cholsey, Berks.**

Dear Margaret, Thank you for your letter.

I will try to let you hear definitely something of our prospects by the end of this week, the 3rd or 4th July. I don't think for a moment that Italy will want us, so I am going to town tomorrow to try to arrange the Argonne thing*. It will probably be very rough and ready, and we shall be, if it is arranged, the annexe of an existing hospital, of whose personnel I can know nothing till I have visited them. If we go, I think we should like you and Miss Hamersley to be our cooks and caterers, as there has been a fearful row with our proposed kitchen staff and I believe they have withdrawn. If you have any other capable friend, please enlist her, or him, when we know what is to be. Tomorrow, as usual in these cases we begin again at the good old departmental play of interviewing twenty people so as to get a twenty first to telegraph. Lucky you, to be really at work.

We all greet you and send you our best remembrances and wish very much that you were walking over the downs to us at this minute. After the war I hope we shall often see you. I will telegraph good news: in fact I had better telegraph any news, for I have kept you and Miss Hamersley a long time. The authorities say that they replied to our first offer within 3 days, but that some official at the Embassy never delivered the message, and so four weeks were lost, 8 lives and perhaps 16 limbs and 32 weeks of suffering.

Most friendly greetings from us all.

Yours very sincerely   *John Masefield*

4 *Sunday night, 25 July*   *Boulogne*

Dear Mr Masefield, I am so *very* glad that it is settled about the Hospital and am most anxious to hear further. Our Office is coming to an end and I am coming home on Wednesday and shall look forward to seeing you soon. Miss Hamersley is ready to come as soon as everything is definitely settled, but I don't want her to leave her present job if there is still any uncertainty. I also have a new job offered to me here, which is being kept open for me until I hear definitely from you. Miss H and I came down to the Quay and waited hoping to see you. I was very sorry to miss you. I am most excited to learn further news and details. I am glad to be coming home and shall not really mind a rest.

Yours very sincerely   *Margaret Bridges*

Lollingdon Downs

I

So I have known this life,
These beads of coloured days,
This self the string.
What is this thing?

Not beauty; no; not greed,
O, not indeed;
Not all, though much;
Its colour is not such.

It has no eyes to see,
It has no ears,
It is a red hour's war
Followed by tears.

It is an hour of time,
An hour of road,
Flesh is its goad,
Yet, in the sorrowing lands,
Women and men take hands.

O earth, give us the corn,
Come rain, come sun,
We men who have been born
Have tasks undone.
Out of this earth
Comes the thing birth,
The things unguessed, unwon.

II

O wretched man, that, for a little mile,
Crawls beneath heaven for his brother's blood,
Whose days the planets number with their style,
To whom all earth is slave, all living, food;

O withering man, within whose folded shell
Lies yet the seed, the spirit's quickening corn,

That Time and Sun will change out of the cell
Into green meadows, in the world unborn;

If Beauty be a dream, do but resolve
And fire shall come, that in the stubborn clay
Works to make perfect till the rocks dissolve,
The barriers burst and Beauty takes her way,

Beauty herself, within whose blossoming Spring
Even wretched man shall clap his hands and sing.

III

You are the link which binds us each to each.
Passion, or too much thought, alone can end
Beauty, the ghost, the spirit's common speech,
Which man's red longing left us for our friend.

Even in the blinding war I have known this,
That flesh is but the carrier of a ghost
Who, through his longing, touches that which is
Even as the sailor knows the foreign coast.

So, by the bedside of the dying black
I felt our uncouth souls subtly made one,
Forgiven, the meanness of each other's lack,
Forgiven, the petty tale of ill things done.

We were but Man, who for a tale of days
Seeks the one city by a million ways.

5   *18 January*   *13 Well Walk, London, NW**

My dear Margaret, Thank you so very much for your letter and for all the trouble you have taken for us and for your kind lifts to and from Oxford on Tuesday. Many thanks for all these things, which have made even house hunting a pleasure. Foxcombe Villa is too expensive, though no doubt they would abate their greedy claims if one were bloody and bold with them; I expect they would come down £200. Our present thought is: perhaps the Trustees or people will let us Hill Crest* for 3 years, with the option of purchase, and if so, we shall take it (I expect) and move into it at once, if we can, with our Lollingdon furniture, and let this house, furnished, as some Australians seem eager to take it. Then, in about a year, we shall start for America, provided we aren't strafed before then, and when we come back, have our London furniture brought up and really settle in.

We feel that probably we could not buy Hill Crest at the present moment, because that would mean selling out securities on a low market, and, I suppose, pawning my plate and other horrors. Still, we now wait on what the Trustees decide. Perhaps, if we take Hill Crest, we shall change the name to Judith's* phrase: Sticky Limit: 'This jam is the Sticky Limit. This place is the Sticky Limit.' We shall be very glad to consult with Mr Waterhouse* on the possibilities of the house. I expect that we could make it nice. With the Bridges household* so near, and peace coming 'O wilderness were Paradise enow.'

Only you will have to come to stay with us just as you did at Lollingdon.

We are very glad that your Mother is so much better. Con* asks me to thank her for her very kind offer of a bed. I expect to go to France on Monday. After that, if the Trustees are at all forthcoming, I daresay Con would like to come down pretty soon.

Lewis*, who is a staunch Churchman, and gives all his toy rabbits communion service daily, and cuffs them good lusty bangs if they try to drink all the wine at one go, as they are wont, asks anxiously 'how far is it to the Church?' I say 'a good way,' though I don't really know, but that 'there are many Churches in Oxford.' For some reason he believes that a Harvest Thanksgiving in Oxford is a pageant of surpassing splendour, and he looks forward to it.

I've read a good chunk of *Mr Britling**, and admire some of his shrewdness very much. He puts a very neat and sure finger on a lot of raw places; and yet, the war moves our minds so fast, that one keeps feeling 'Yes; we did think that, say, 6 months ago; but all sorts of things have happened since then; it is old-fashioned now: we are past that.'

Please let me know where you go, and let us look forward to being neighbours. All good wishes to you for a very happy and successful time in France and all thanks to you and all of you for so much kindness and niceness and help.

Always yours sincerely   *John Masefield*

My little play, of Good Friday*, is to be done by the Stage Society about Feb. 19th. Would any of you care to come for it, if we are still here? I shall be away and Con could put you up.

6   *26 February*   *1(d), GHQ, BEF*

My dear Margaret, I did not expect to see you yesterday, as it was such a muggy evening; but I shall hope to be able to see you when I leave, if not before.

How did you get across, and how have you settled down, and what sort of an orderly have they given you this time? I hope he is as good an one as the last, and that he will have a light hand with pastry.

I hope that the change has quite cured your throat.

This place* is like Arc-en-Barrois* where I was in hospital; a flat sort of beaver meadow, with a clear oolite river, rather rapid and full of trout, running through it, and a steep wooded scarp above. The château is down on the flat, and I am billetted near it in the village.

We were so very glad to have you for a few hours before you sailed; and what a pity you did not stay on and come across with me (as things turned out).

Probably you will not have any sort of time for writing without giving up some of your time for being in the open air, so will you let the arrangement be that my letters will not need a reply, or only a reply on a postcard, so that then I shall feel that I am not robbing you of a walk or a swim.

Con goes to Oxford tomorrow, to see Sandpits.

All good wishes and greetings to you, I hope that you will have a very happy jolly time. Always yours sincerely   *John Masefield*

7   *1 March*   *CWL Hur, APO 5.18, BEF*

Dear Mr Masefield, I got your telegram on Sunday morning and went down on the Quay at 1 oclock to find when the boat should be in. There was one just coming in then, and I waited one hour while they disembarked thinking that you might be on it. I came over here (which is [blotted or censored]) on Sunday afternoon and I shall be here for a week or so before settling down as cook at Boulogne. No cooking here, but barmaid work. I was here before a little over a year ago and am glad to be back here again. They are short-handed here at present and the old cook at Boulogne has not yet left. This is a very pleasant camp here. There is a great deal of work, but I am settling down to it comfortably and thoroughly enjoying it. We have had a grand scrimmage tonight, as it is Pay-Day. I heard from Edward* this morning, but he didn't say if he had been in any of the recent fighting. My steamer collided with a mine-sweeper on the way over. We stopped to pick up 2 of the crew of the mine-sweeper who were swept overboard. Our bows were crumpled up like a piece of paper. It was fortunately calm.

I did enjoy being with you at Hampstead and wished it had not been so short and hurried, and also that you had not paid for my taxi! Thank you *very* much for being so very very kind. I can't write sense as everybody else is counting 5-franc notes, and I must now go to bed.

I shall look forward to hearing from you when you have time, and to hearing a little about your work if you may write about it.

Please forgive such a scribble.

 Yours very sincerely   *Margaret Bridges*

We have an orderly who was a keeper in Epping Forest!

Edward Bridges

8   *5 March*   *1(d), GHQ, BEF*

My dear Margaret, Though this is still my address, I am at the
moment away from it, in a billet at Albert,* which will probably
soon be my permanent quarters. I pass my days wandering over
the battlefield, where the camps and dumps have now almost
changed it out of all knowledge, except where the fighting has
been recent. Some of the mess and desolation must be seen to be
believed, but there is a kind of romance in some of it. Thiepval*
and the horrible redoubts beyond it have a kind of splendid

horror over them, as though the soul of man really reached a limit in them; which is something. Today, when I saw them, there was a partly melted snow on them, and gloom overhead, so that they were at their deepest, and no birds were there. There were plenty of helmets (for Elizabeth*) but I didn't like the looks of them, so did not bring one. I am however bringing you a few little things, noses of shells, shrapnel, éclats, etc. There were several broken Tanks, one of them with the legend on it, 'The Bing Boys are here'. Alas, I'm afraid they were there, poor fellows, when the thing went over.

I can't get used to these thoughts; they break my heart wherever I go here. I came across a lonely grave today with a packing-case cross over it, and a pencilled inscription on the cross, In loving memory of Pte J. Redhead. Killed in action Sept 16 and the knowledge that the man must have been called Ginger made it full of pathos. There was another lonely grave with 2 words on it: Dead Fritz.

There may be some special kind of trophy which you greatly covet, and if there be, will you let me know what it is? Edward would probably get you finer things than I, but with two seekers you might be more certain of getting what you want.

I cannot bring you rifles or explosives; but what I can I will bring.

I hope that you are set up and settled down now, and liking the work and the people.

They bomb here a good deal. I hope you are spared that.

All happy pleasant prosperous fortune to you and the best of good wishes. Always yours very sincerely   *John Masefield*

9   *6 March*   *CWL Hur, APO 5.18, BEF*

Dear Mr Masefield, I'm afraid they will be clearing Edward out [blotted or censored] as soon as his temperature has been normal in the evening he will be sent to England. It was 101 last night, but was expected to be much lower tonight, so that probably Wed. or Thurs. will see him packed off. So by the time you get this he will probably be gone.

I only write to tell you this in case you were thinking of getting over. In haste   Yrs   *Margaret Bridges*

10   *10 March*   *1(d), GHQ*

My dear Margaret, Thank you very much indeed for writing to me about Edward. I am dreadfully concerned to hear the news and think of all your distress. It is miserable and terrible, but I do hope to God that the arm will be saved, and that he himself will not suffer much. I feel most deeply for your anxiety and trouble; and for this to come just after the house is most cruel. You would all have been so happy, nursing him there. I wish that I could come over to see you, and perhaps Edward, too; but there is no chance of that. I only got your letters this morning.

It was most kind and good of you to send me word about him. This is just a note, to say how very very sorry I am, and to wish you, and Edward too, a happy end of it. Give him all my greetings and tell him to cheer up. All my greetings to you both. It will be most kind if you can let me know how he goes on. Perhaps you will be going home to nurse him? This may seem an unfeeling note, it is written so hurriedly, but I feel it deeply, and so will Con.

Bless you. Yours always sincerely   *John Masefield*

11   *18 March*   *1(d), c/o RTO, BEF, Amiens*

My dear Margaret, Thank you so much for your letter of the 12th (received today, as I have been changed to here). It was most awfully good of you to write to tell me of Edward, and I am glad and happy to think that he is going on well and that he will be out of it for some months at least. It is jolly good news to all of us; for I am sure no day has passed, since he went out, that we have not thought anxiously of him, for his sake and for yours. I hope my dear Margaret that you will hear nothing but good news of him now that he is back in Blighty* and that you will have a happy time with him when you go home. You will have to go to Con at Sandpits with him.

I am staying at Amiens this week, at the above address, which is my postal address, and then (as far as I know) go to live again in Albert, which is rather a wonderful place, much smashed, but rather grand, like the gateway to much that was great and terrible. Only 2 days ago I was just below Bapaume*, and saw a German squad marching in Le Tramsloy, and now they are gone and away and will never be back again.

The battlefield is a bedevilled and desolate and awful place, still heaped, here and there, with dead Germans, and all littered and skinned and gouged, till it looks like the country of the moon. Here there is a heap of picks, there a coil of wire, here a body or a leg, then a bomb or two, a rifle, a smashed helmet, a few dozen cartridges, then some boots with feet in them, a mess of old coats and straps and leather work, all smashed and smothered in a litter of mud and mess, and great big stinking pools and old dud shells, burnt trees, and powdered bricks and iron. It cannot be described nor imagined; but I suppose the place once looked like the Chilterns, and now, at a distance, it looks like Dartmoor under rain, and nearby like Sodom and Gomorrah.

Near the ruins of Hamel there is a little dwarf evergreen which somehow hasn't been destroyed. A soldier has put a notice on it: Kew Gardens. Please do not touch.

Alas, alas, for all my fine hopes of coming to visit you. It is too far and cannot be done.

Bless you my dear Margaret. I hope truly with all my heart that Edward is getting on well. All greetings and good wishes to him and to you. Always yours very sincerely   *John Masefield*

12   *23 March*   *l(d), BEF, Amiens*

My dear Margaret, I'm afraid that letters do not arrive anywhere when posted, as this will be, from Albert, where I now am; but one never knows. This one may get through to you.

I hope that you have good news of Edward and that you aren't feeling the loneliness too much, now that you have the strain of worrying about him added to it. If this ever reaches you and you have a moment to answer it, will you let me know, if you are on a telephone? and if so, what your number is, and what time you could be rung up; for when I get back to Amiens, I could ring you up every day that I am there; and that would be a great pleasure to me, if you would not mind, and some atonement for not seeing you at Boulogne and not being able to come to see you afterwards.

There was a telephone here, but some officer pinched it yesterday (cut it off and pocketed it): I can't think why; but some people are specially sensitive to certain things. Major Griffiths said that he once knew a thief who could be trusted with money and jewels, but could not be left alone with a garden roller.

Spring is beginning on the battlefield. I counted two coltsfoots today. It is a late spring and all this field is so blasted that it is still doubtful whether anything will grow on it. I hope that the spring will cover it all, all these poor heads and bodies lying loose in the shell holes and on the mole hills, so that one may feel them to be taken to the earth instead of cast out from it.

Con moves into Sandpits about next Wednesday. You will have to come to us there often.

All good wishes to you. I hope that you have a good orderly and that the soldiers like your dishes as much as they always did.

All greetings. Always yours very sincerely   *John Masefield*

It seems that I heard the last German shell on this place. Now they are quite out of range.

13   *29 March*   *l(d), BEF, Amiens*

My dear Margaret, So many thanks for your letter and card. It was very good of you to bother to write to me when you were ill, and I am so sorry to think of you being laid up in this foreign land and hope that you are now well and about again. We are all very anxious about Edward; don't add to our troubles by your falling ill.

I am awfully glad that Edward is going on well. Do not fret about him more than you must, for all must be going well now that his temperature is down, and he back in Blighty. Con is (I'm afraid) moving in to Sandpits in these days, or I would get her to go to visit Edward and then write to you about him. But as that cannot be, I can only say cheer up, as I'm sure things are going well with him, and it cannot be long before he will be able to write to you.

This isn't a letter, as a man is playing the piano, and 20 officers, English and French, all talking at once, half of them to me, are at my elbow gabbling about the war and poetry and the use of artillery. It seems that there is a new stuff, called porridge, for destroying Zeppelins, which is A1.

I'll try to write you a proper letter tomorrow, for I hate to send you a note like this, when you are ill and so worried and troubled. Let me know, will you, if you are short of things to read, though you have little time for reading, I know.

Cheer up, and bless you for writing.

Yours sincerely   *John Masefield*

14   *29 March*

My dear Margaret, I could not write you a letter this evening, as the room was full of noise just before post, but will try to write now, in the comparative peace of bed.

I went into Peronne on Sunday; a very beautiful day and beautiful place; we went over roads where we'd been shelled only a week before, and then came down to the Somme, quite a lovely quiet little river there, or rather a collection of blue pools, with reeds and water hens. Presently we came out of Clery, all smashed to bits, to the enemy lines, just as he had left them, all his wire intact (miles of it) and all his nice dug-outs full of booby traps, corked rum-jars, nice revolvers, helmets etc, which, if you lift them explode mines and blow you to pieces (this being German wit) and any amount of litter, old tins, German books, letters, postcards, and hand grenades really by the hundred, barbed-wire coils, trench-mortar-bombs, and neat wooden plaques each saying that something was forbidden. He had had to go back from those lines quicker than he meant, for by the road were lots of trees which he had begun to cut through so that they might fall across the road, but had then had to leave.

Peronne is surrounded by a clear running chalk stream moat, and old Vauban fortifications, and there is an old château, too strong for him to smash, but much knocked about. The town itself must have been a very beautiful quiet decent little well-built French city, but think what these creatures had done to it. They had pulled out the front from pretty nearly every house, and what they hadn't pulled down they had blasted or mined. Then they had gathered practically every scrap and stick and chattel out of the houses and laid it all in the open, had stolen and sent away all that they liked or could carry and had then smashed, defaced, or defiled everything that remained. The little cathedral, which must once have been truly lovely, they blew up by a mine, and then, having cut every fruit tree in every garden, they went away. It was a lovely sunny day when we saw all this, and the sight of all this order and niceness and beauty, all lit up in its defilement, made the heart ache. By the way, on the plinth of a statue (statue gone of course) were chalked the numbers of the battalions which had taken the city, and Edward's old battalion* was third on the list.

Your letter and card reached me this Thursday evening together.

I have been seeing a lot of Anzacs* up near the line, and they are a fine lot of men, easily the finest men fighting on this front, and by much the cleverest and most daring fighters. They are handsome and brave and clever, and most beautiful on horses; you can tell them by their riding half a mile away. It is the kind of life they lead that makes them such men. They are the likest men to sailors in their manliness, and much better than sailors in their generosity and niceness of mind.

I also saw Rupert Brooke's battalion*, but oh how changed; all the old Gallipoli men gone, except 2 or 3, and the rest young lads, but still led by the daredevil Freyberg*, who swam the great swim with the flares at Xeros Bay in Gallipoli. He is a New Zealander, too, and is only 29, and is a Colonel and a VC an MC and a DSO and has been 5 times wounded.

By the way, here is a curio for you. It is one of the franc notes issued in the captured towns during the enemy occupation. You may already have some of them, but if you have not, perhaps it may amuse you to have it.

I hope you will have lots of good news and letters from Edward. Poor Con I'm afraid is now moving house. Would I were there to help her.

All good wishes. Always yours sincerely   *John Masefield*

I hope your cold and throat are quite cured and that your cooking is again the joy of the wounded.

Sonnets

Here, where we stood together, we three men,
Before the war had swept us to the East
Three thousand miles away, I stand again
And hear the bells, and breathe, and go to feast.
We trod the same path, to the self-same place,
Yet here I stand, having beheld their graves,
Skyros whose shadows the great seas erase,
And Seddul Bahr that ever more blood craves.
So, since we command here, our bones have been
Nearer, perhaps, than they again will be,
Earth and the world-wide battle lie between,
Death lies between, and friend-destroying sea.
Yet here, a year ago, we talked and stood
As I stand now, with pulses beating blood.

I saw her like a shadow on the sky
In the last light, a blur upon the sea,
Then the gale's darkness put the shadow by,
But from one grave that island talked to me;
And, in the midnight, in the breaking storm,
I saw its blackness and a blinking light,
And thought, 'So death obscures your gentle form,
So memory strives to make the darkness bright;
And, in that heap of rocks, your body lies,
Part of the island till the planet ends,
My gentle comrade, beautiful and wise,
Part of this crag this bitter surge offends,
While I, who pass, a little obscure thing,
War with this force, and breathe, and am its king.'

Time being an instant in eternity,
Beauty above man's million years must see
The heaped corrupted mass that had to die,
The husk of man that set the glitter free;
Now from those million bodies in the dark,
Forgotten, rotten, part of fields or roads,
The million gleam united makes a spark

Which Beauty sees among her star abodes.
And, from the bodies, comes a sigh, 'Alas,
We hated, fought and killed, as separate men;
Now all is merged and we are in the grass,
Our efforts merged, would we had known it then.
All our lives' battle, all our spirits' dream,
Nought in themselves, a clash which made a gleam.'

15   *3 April*   *l(d), (rue Jules Lardière), BEF, Amiens*

My dear Margaret, I am so awfully sorry to hear that you have been laid up, and do hope that you are better and not having a bad time. And I do wish that I had known sooner, it is wretched luck; for I would have sent you some books, and written, and done what I could, for it must have been most mouldy for you, ill alone in camp. But your letter took 6 days to get here, as the RTO was puzzled: I don't know why. If you write again soon, as I hope you will, to say that you are well, will you put (rue Jules Lardière) in brackets on the envelope; that will take all doubts from his mind, and the letter may come to me in a day or two.

I hope you are well now, really well, and not too bored and tired. I do wish your letter had come sooner, but still, it has come, and I am awfully sorry to think of you being ill and alone.

All greetings and good wishes and, as Lady Macbeth says, not I, 'Out, out, d—d spots.' Yours   *John Masefield*

16   *4 April*   *l(d), c/o RTO Amiens*

My dear Margaret, I am so very very sorry for you; how wretched for poor you. I hope it hasn't been too thin a time, alone and ill and in a cubicle, with nothing to read, and no letters from Edward, (and probably none from anyone else, since the cross country posts go from bad to worse now). Your letter only reached me last night, or I would have sent you some things to read. Now you are well I hope and off to Boulogne again. Let me have a card, will you, if you have time, to say if you are well, and where you are.

I sent you a note last night to Wimereux and am now writing this (in bed in the early morning) so that you may get it reasonably soon at Boulogne.

I did not answer your question about the Russians, I'm afraid. The general feeling here, is that Russia as a whole is in a critical way, but that the revolution will probably be in our favour, and may be enormously so, if only as an object lesson to Germany. There are some hints, very vague, and not yet to be taken seriously, of simmerings in western Germany, aiming at detachment from Prussia; but these are not likely to lead to much. The Russian coup* succeeded because three fifths of the able-bodied men are not yet in the army, while in western Germany the Prussian system has caught them all.

The latest haul of prisoners here included the maimed, the halt, the imbecile and the blind; they were like Falstaff's squad. I think this means that they are not going to fight just here, but to hold us, if they can, with cripples and machines, while they put every man and gun against Italy, and perhaps Holland, too.

This is only a note of condolence, not a letter. I do wish that I had heard of your illness sooner, so that I could have written every day and sent you things. All good wishes now anyway for a complete recovery. It is glorious that Edward is going on well.

Yours always   *John Masefield*

17   *4 April*

My dear Margaret, Poor you with the measles, or only just out of them, fill me with sympathy and sorrow. I have rummaged around for a few books, but such a mouldy set one never did see, except in an English town like Wolverhampton or Leicester. Still I do hope that such as they are they will while away a few of your hours of convalescence. The de Vigny* is very perfect but a little dull, rather wanting in wildness; it is like, if I may say so without committing *lèse-majesté*, or interfering with recruiting, a little like a British General Head Quarters, as compared with an Australian one. The Conrad Romance I used to like, but haven't read for many years. Huck Finn is the one masterpiece America has yet produced, and though you probably know it well, I was so glad to see it on the shelf that I couldn't resist it; do tell me if you like it awfully. It is the one wonderful book about boyhood. *Tom Sawyer* is nearly as good, but Huck has this vast romantic setting of the Mississipi [sic] River. The Valerie book is said to be a study of a female prig, and the Anatole is quite slight, but rather charming.

There were no Dostoievskys or other Russians, and only one Wells, so I could not send you anything really after your heart. Even these which I send will probably be a week on their way to you.

Tell me about your measles. Judith had the same kind at school this term, and from what she said they are the mildest things I have heard about the Hun for years. Are you spotty at first and do you peel, or are they sometimes severe? I'm afraid you had rather a sharp attack, with throat and fever. Judith had a school attack, with cake, oranges and chocolate cream.

Dostoievsky never exactly wins me, but he certainly haunts me, though not in the way of beauty; in the way, more, of the mad man whom one sees in a cell. Don't you think that the really haunting things come from the imaginations of the many (popular tales and traditions) suddenly made significant by the brooding of one great imagination? D strikes me as a hurt thing, who says 'I don't know any tales or traditions; I only know this thing, whatever it is, called Human Life, with all these things called Human Institutions arrayed against it, and it hurts and hurts, and there is no escape from it; it is too wonderful to escape from; and this is how it has to live, and it is awful.'

Do you ever read Anatole France*? He was probably never much hurt by life and he seems an exceedingly comfortable caustic soul, doing himself exceedingly well, with a nice dejeuner and then a mock at the church, and then a nice diner and a dissection of a nerve. His instrument is the nerve, and when he really gets on to the nerve he has a kind of naked horror that is quite awful. Do tell me if you have read much of him and what you think of him, and if you have ever read one of his terrible tales, like l'*Histoire Comique**? He has a way of making a novel an entire social history (in his lighter veins), but his terrible tales are the things one remembers: all Frenchmen seem able to be light.

On Sunday I was out not far from Bapaume, and one of our sausage observation balloons went up, and hadn't been up 5 minutes before a Boche aeroplane came up, under a heavy fire, bombed it and set it on fire and then fled. The 2 observers hopped out of the flames and down by parachute, and I think were both saved, but could not quite see. The poor old sausage was ashes in ten seconds, in one vast blast of fire which burnt it all, and the Boche man, who was a jolly dashing soul, got clean away. The whole thing took about 20 seconds. Afterwards I went to Peronne and saw little Poincare* giving medals to some English officers and (to their great relief) not trying to kiss them as Joffre used to.

Bless you, and I hope you are well now. Yours   *John Masefield*

America is 'in'.* It may lead to a greater unity in those very Disunited States, but I expect the Boche will raise too much trouble in Mexico to let her help much over here, except financially and possibly by shipping. She gets ½ a million tons of Boche shipping at a stroke, worth about ten million pounds or more; which is pleasant to think of. All greetings.

18 *11 April*

My dear Margaret, I am so glad to hear of your being better and having some sort of time for rest. Poor you; I'm afraid you had a miserable time, and I hate to think of the throat, too; and I do hope my dear Margaret that that is over now and that it didn't hurt too much, and that now it is well. You shall have some more books in a few days time. You must let me do that, for you know we always talk and think of you as one of ourselves, a quite specially intimate, and it is such a pleasure to go a-hunting for you, in the rubbish of these shops. I'll get you an Anatole*; one of the historical novels; about the Revolution, with guillotine complete, as that is rather a good one.

It is jolly good news about Edward; thank you so much for thinking to tell me. Poor Con and Nana are down at Loll in the cold, waiting till the snow melts, so that they can get the lorries up the lane to move them to Oxford. Lew is in London waiting till they are moved.

Yesterday I went to one of the HQs to see some English soldiers who had been prisoners with the Germans for 3 months and had then got away. They were both covered with boils, from underfeeding and lowered power of resistance, and the elder of the 2 men (a third was in hospital) had 3 frostbitten toes. They had been put to sleep in an old brick kiln, with no blankets, during all the cold of this winter, and they were worked on the roads 8 hours a day, and no matter how ill they were they were beaten out to work with whips, and knocked about with rifle-butts if they paused during working hours. They had only one meal a day, of a quarter of a loaf of bread and 'a bit of meat as big as a lump of sugar,' and they ate this in the mornings, 'so as to have something to work on,' and they had nothing else except 2 cups of thin soup and 1 cup of coffee, and they used to get so mad with hunger that they would eat rotten turnips and old frosted potatoes when they could find them, and be very glad of them. The Germans paid them 2 francs 80 for ten days work, and paid them in cardboard money (which they shewed me — yellow scraps of cardboard about as big as ladies' visiting cards, with type written values on them) and then as soon as the poor fellows were paid, the Germans used to mock them, and say, 'You needn't think you can buy anything with your money; you can't'; and of course they couldn't, the cards were worthless. At last, 3 of them slipped away, one of these last moonlit nights, and got across 2 German trenches full of men, walking towards the flashes of the English guns. (*They* were walking I mean; not the German trenches.) They were challenged at the second trench, and the man who challenged them was unarmed, and ran away calling to his mates, and I hope got clouted on the head by his sergeant for making such a row. The three got across to the Hindenburg Line, which was only held by sentries, and a sentry saw them and fired and shot one of them through the shoulder. But it was only a light wound, and they managed to cross the wire (8 rows, 5 yards wide) by walking on the top of it, it being so stout and thick that it was like a paved road. Fritz always was lavish of his wire, and here he seems to have surpassed himself, though I cannot see why they weren't seen and killed.

Presently they crossed No Man's Land and the Australians took them in. They had had no wash for 3 months, as they were given no soap nor any change of clothes by the Germans, and had received no letters nor parcels of any kind, and had only been allowed to send 3 cards home in all that time, and they felt that even these were never sent. Altogether it was a pretty evil story of cruelty and dirty devilry done to poor men.

Thank you so much for your jolly letter and card. Let me have a card, will you, when you can, to say if the throat is better, and if there is anything I could get or do for you. I'm afraid books and letters are about all my kingdom and power here. I'll write again in a day or two, for I may hear tales of this new attack before long, and they might amuse you.

I wish I could think your throat were well in this cold winter weather. All greetings and good wishes to you.

Always yours   *John Masefield*

19   *12 April*

My dear Margaret, I find that the Revolution book cannot be here for a fortnight, so that you will hardly get it till the end of the month. However you shall have something instead of it within a few days.

The battle of Arras* was very successful. We have a new gas, it seems, which is efficacious. Only two years ago the enemy started gas at Ypres*, and made his road clear, but perhaps did not then trust his chemists enough; anyhow he did not follow up his success. Then we shouted, 'Dastardly outrage, inhuman devilry, the Hun out-hunned.' Now we say, 'Triumph of British Science, our chemists lead us to victory, the new gas kills the Hun through his respirator.'

One Canadian Brigade took 33 guns. They attacked in the dark and entrenched themselves in their new position at about midnight, and when it dawned they saw a long gun position full of cannon within 200 yards of them, so they rushed it and took all the guns in it.

The enemy is said not to have fought so well as he fought on the Somme, but then our artillery was infinitely more awful. Lots of the enemy were starving, as no food had come to them for 8 days (nothing could get through the barrage), and these surrendered readily, and are now at work on our roads. On one dead German they found a certificate of naturalisation as an American citizen, 'renouncing all allegiance to William II'.

I've been thinking of your poor throat, and poor you generally in this cold weather not at all well. I hope you are mending and that the cautery is over and was not painful, and I hope you aren't brooding and worrying over Edward too much and feeling the loneliness a lot. I'm afraid you may be having a very thin time, and that makes me sad for you.

Wheeled stretchers take the wounded from the firing-line

Do you know Amiens at all? It has an old squalid distorted nightmare quarter, built in the Middle Ages, with rushing rivers instead of streets; it is all like a cramped and twisted mind given to devilry. One of the paved streets is called 'the street of the Naked Corpse without a Head'. All this devilry and grinnery and distortion is like what one loved and was afraid of as a child. And little distorted urchins and shrill ladies come out of street corners and say 'Godam' at you as you pass. Sometimes nowadays they call us 'Jesuschrists'; so perhaps our stock stands higher in the market than it did. Once a factory came out from work as I passed, and every bright lady in it hailed me as one or the other.

All good wishes, from   *John Masefield*

20   *13 April*

My dear Margaret, This is just a line, to say, that I have been today in Hébuterne*, where Edward was for so long.

He will have told you all about it, and I expect it hasn't much changed since he was there. It is almost deserted now. Two lonely soldiers were collecting barbed wire and German bombs there. We put up a hare and some partridges in the No Man's Land; and the enemy trenches have nothing but rats in them now. The enemy had a vast stronghold there, opposite Edward, with trenches 15 feet deep in places, and 30 yards of wire in front of them, and ten yards of trip wire in front of that, and concealed machine guns in front of that.

Sad heaps of our men were everywhere. In places they lay in whole platoons, Durhams and Londons and London Scottish, all along the line, just as they fell on July 1st*. It was the saddest place I have seen on the whole field.

I hope the throat goes on towards recovery.

Con is still at Loll.

Best wishes and good luck to you.

Always yours sincerely   *John Masefield*

21   *14 April*

My dear Margaret, Your letter just now came. I'm most awfully sorry and concerned to hear your news. My poor Margaret I am most awfully sorry and anxious, to think of you ill and in pain and in a sort of beer house with people celebrating no les. [sic] Dear Margaret I hope truly your MO is looking after you and seeing that some nice people look after you too. I do wish I could help. Is there anybody I could write to, or anything I could do for you?

I wish I could pull some strings, so as to make sure that you are really looked after; one feels so helpless out here like this. I was afraid you were ill.

This is a very hurried scrap to catch the post. Be sure to take care of yourself. I'll write to you every day I can, don't trouble to answer, as writing is a labour and you are ill.

All blessings and comforts fall upon you and make you speedily well. Yours always   *John Masefield*

22   *15 April*

My dear Margaret, Here is an Anatole*, a very popular one, which I've neither read nor heard of, so don't know what is in it. I've run it through with scissors, to save you the bother of cutting, but don't know what it is about, though he seems to be having a go at the Jews in it and perhaps Church and State as well. If it is one of his witty and shrewd books it may amuse you; if it is one of his terrors please forgive me for sending it. Alas, you may be back in Blighty before it reaches you; though indeed I ought not to say alas, for I wish I could think of you as already there, being properly looked after. Anyhow, I hope the pain is less sharp and that you aren't feeling too miserable and that people are being nice and gentle about you and trying to get you well.

All good wishes, Always sincerely yours   *John Masefield*

The MO is quite right. 'Blighty is the place for you' just now.

23   *16 April*

My dear Margaret, I could not write you a proper letter yesterday, though I wanted to, for I was out all day until after the post had gone. I could only send you a line with a copy of an Anatole France, which I hope isn't one of his outrageous ones. How are you now? I do hope better, and I do hope everybody is being nice and helpful and friendly to you. You may be away by this time for Blighty, but I don't know enough about pleurisy to be sure of this. One good thing about your going will be, that you will be able to see a great deal of Edward, and have a jolly happy time of getting well together, and it is very nice to think that you will have that happiness. I've told Con that you are going to England; she is still at Loll, as far as I can make out, for the roads there are too muddy for the furniture vans, and she is waiting for them to dry up, but she may have moved since my last letter. As soon as she is in Sandpits (it will be about the time you can go gadding about again) you will be a most trebly welcome visitor, so will you propose yourself, and go there, if you feel able for it and can spare the time from Edward? Do, if you can.

In this scattered sort of life I can't remember what I have said in previous letters. Did I tell you of the Australian soldier? The Australian Pioneers wear a badge, of a rifle crossed with a spade, which looks very like the Br General's badge of 2 crossed swords. A Br General was passing an Australian sentry and the sentry didn't salute. The General in a mild way of sarcasm asked, 'Don't you even salute a general?' The man saluted and said, 'I took you for one of them Pioneers and I wasn't going to salute one of them swine.'

In the fighting on the Cambrai road the other day, an Australian patrol of 9 men had a fight with about 30 Germans, and killed and wounded a lot of them. Then the Germans brought up a machine gun and killed 3 of them and wounded 4, which left only 2 (in case the pleurisy makes your head at all cloudy) and these 2 hid in a shell hole. The Germans having won the victory began to look after their wounded, and while they were busy doing this, these 2 unwounded Australians crept out of the shell hole and sneaked their machine gun. They didn't know how to work it, or they might have captured and killed all the Germans, but they picked it up and crawled away and brought it back into our lines.

The Germans have still a very excellent intelligence department. I have seen some translations of captured letters, which shew that they expected the Arras attack, and knew exactly what troops were going to make it, but they expected it to come some days before it actually came. In particular details, they are less well-informed. They did not know how many batteries we had, nor where they were placed, and the hell of fire that came upon them was a surprise to them, even after the Somme. I believe the battle brought down upon them something like 80,000 tons of shells, not to speak of bullets and bombs, and the letters found on the dead and prisoners describe it as more awful than any thing they had ever imagined or experienced before.

I believe the French are having a push in this next day or two, so perhaps the enemy may not be able to make his attack in Italy after all. He saved some 6 or 7 divisions by shortening his line here, and it is thought that the saved troops will be put in against Italy. He might put them in against Russia, but the distances there are very great.

What do you think the US will do? I wonder if a million 'live' Americans could treble the Siberian line, get through munitions to the Eastern front, and have a million men there by Xmas. I don't think that they will be anything like as swift as we were, for they are really a slow moving people, though they think themselves quick; but they are very courageous and very inventive and oh my dear Margaret think what joy, if they could furnish us with a princess, just new out of Bryn Mawr, with the chewing gum minty on her lips, for our young prince to marry.

All good wishes and I do hope your pain is gone.

Always yours sincerely   *John Masefield*

24 *17 April*   *No 1 Convalescent Camp, Boulogne*

Dear Mr Masefield, Thank you for two letters, and for all your kind sympathy. Yours of the 16th has just come, which is wonderfully quick. The story of the Australian sentry and the Br. General made me laugh very much.

Yes, I am *very* glad to think that I am going to be within reach of Edward. I am afraid that he will be kept in bed in London for some weeks to come, and as I have got to be in the country I shant be able to see much of him. I am *terribly* afraid they won't think me well enough to go gadding up and down to London very often. In fact I am rather dreading the atmosphere of fuss and tender prohibitions that will encircle me directly I reach Yattendon. But it is very ungrateful to say that and I *am very* grateful to have Yattendon to go to.

I seem to write of nothing but myself, but the censorship of our letters is so very strict here that one hardly dares mention the war, and tho' there are one or two things I want to say I think I will postpone them until my return, for my letters have been scratched about twice lately.

I'm hoping to get off on Thursday, but it depends on the size of the boat.

I really am better, and the Pleurisy is behaving well, but feel very good-for-nothing.

The MO has been a bright spot, as he is a proper Doctor with a private practice, a gentleman, and the sort who tells you the truth, as well as being most extraordinarily kind. So I have been fortunate. Now I spend my days in a damp, lugubrious apartment with an evil-smelling stove. A glass door divides me from the billiard room, from whence all day I hear the click of the balls and sundry bilingual conversations. As others are out all day I am pretty much quite alone.

I am afraid Mrs Masefield has been having a poorish time. I shall hope to see her, tho' I have, at present, a foolish dread of going back to Boars Hill and seeing ruined Chilswell. It feels so much a symbol of the ruins of the past. But I can't explain properly what I mean. Yrs   *Margaret Bridges*

25 *27 April*

My dear Margaret, So many thanks for your letter. I am jolly glad to think that you are safely at home, being well looked after; for I was anxious about you. I was afraid you were in for a bad illness. Now I hope you will soon be made as radiant and bonny as you were when you came to Loll in the car in November; and by that time Edward will be about, I hope, and you will have a jolly time together.

I was made very sad by your revelations. It all seems a legacy of a thoroughly vicious system. Something is half done, in a niggardly, unthought-out way, and then a vested interest is created ostensibly as a palliation, but really to perpetuate it. Then something occurs to make the whole thing an outrage, but in a time of such stress that no other machinery can be set up as a substitute, and so the thing goes on, multiplied a thousandfold. The thing seems to go back to our failure in teaching cookery. The French soldier-cooks turn out marvellous meals out of rations really inferior to ours, as I proved at Verdun, time and time again. Our men are driven to buy something with a real taste to it in a canteen, wet or dry. Then the canteen, etc etc.

I must stop now, as I am thick in dust and it is time for mess. Please give my greetings to your Mother. I am jolly glad that she is there to look after you. Always yours sincerely   *John Masefield*

I've been up with the Australians this week, seeing their battle, which is most awful and terrible to hear and see.

American ambulance on shell-swept road near Verdun

26 *11 May*

My dear Margaret, Thank you so much for your letter. I am so awfully glad to think that you and Edward are now getting better. I do trust that you are both out of all pain and able to rest. Thank you so much for writing.

I'm afraid I've not been very punctual in writing to you since you left France, but that is because I've had less time lately. I have been punctual in my thoughts of you, wondering if you were really getting better, and not, as I feared, going to break down. All the spirits of good health surround you, and may you soon be quite heartily and radiantly well again.

Con has great hopes of luring you to her, in spite of the sadness. Do please go, and stay a long time; for if you do, I might just possibly catch you there, for my work here draws to an end.

In some of the recent fighting, a big enemy dugout was taken over by a Brigade HQ and used as such for two days. The dugout had lateral passages leading out of its main room, and one of these passages was blocked by a fall of earth. At the end of two days, one of the staff went exploring beyond this fall of earth with an electric torch, and found three wounded Boche living just beyond it; they had been there all the time and had no doubt enjoyed the Brigade jokes and the discussion of the Brigade plans. One of the Brigade staff told me this, so perhaps it may be true. One of the

Australian stock answers to tellers of similar tales is 'I believe you, though thousands wouldn't.'

We have a Russian here, who is a Revolutionary and has been an exile, and he is a very wise and interesting man. He fought in the Revolution of 1906, and has been a dock labourer in England, as well as a boat-builder and an aeroplane-maker. There have been other Russians here who have been duds, but this man is remarkable. He says, that the German Jews did the harm in Russia, that they got into being Heads of Colleges through the Germanized Court, and that then they simply saw to it that any promising intellect in lad or girl was checked and crushed. He says, that Russia will quite certainly have a kind of offensive in another 2 or 3 weeks, and will stay in the war till the end, but that she may not be able to do very much. His position here among the French is very difficult just now, and they are certainly tactless with him. I expect to be a second to a duel any day, and then 1 or 2 of these French will be killed off, which will do them good, for 1 of them stole my nice gloves the other night, and my blood boils whenever I think of it.

This Russian says that Karalenko* is the man to read. Do you know his books?

Now my dear Margaret I hope when next you write you will say that you are perfectly well and that Edward is with you in the country. Please give my greetings to your Mother, and to Edward. Always yours sincerely   *John Masefield*

27   *18 May*

My dear Margaret, The bookshop people tell me that the Revolution story* is now out of print and cannot be had just yet. This is the Anatole France book I was going to send you, and I tell you this, lest you should think I had forgotten, and should call me a dud, or some other military term.

In a week from today I am to go to Paris, to see some records there, and after a few days there, may be in England again. Do you think you could come to us, if we all promise always to walk you Bagley Wood way?

The Paris records ought to be very strange and sad, for they are said to contain all the available photographs of the towns of the battlefield as they were before the war, so that one may still see what they were, Pozières, which is now 3 mounds and two blocks of concrete, and Mametz, which is eight feet of brick, and Montauban, which is one iron gate, and Longueval, which is a reddish patch on the road, where they put the bricks, and B'mont Hamel which not even the inhabitants can know when they are in it.

I hope that you are really well again and that Edward is now with you. It is nice to think that you will have this time together.

I was asked out to tea last Sunday, that is, to port wine and cake, by a French family, who afterwards sang 'Who's your lady friend?' to me, to shew that they knew the English taste. Then afterwards they sang an old French nursery rhyme to a very lovely tune:

> Au clair de la lune
> Mon ami Pierrot
> Prêtes moi ta plume   etc

which I do hope you know and will someday play to us; it is quite beautiful.

Last week a man of one of our patrols was out in No Man's Land for four days. When he came in, an officer asked him, why he hadn't come in with the rest of the patrol. He said, 'There was too much shell fire the first two days, sir,' The officer asked, why he didn't come in on the 3rd day. The man said, 'There was too much machine-gun fire, sir,' 'Well,' said the officer.

But I told you this story last week, while it was still fresh, now that I come to think of it.

I must go to dress for mess and also to put a patch in a garment for the same.

All good wishes to you. Always yours sincerely   *John Masefield*

The Downland

Night is on the downland, on the lonely moorland,
On the hills where the wind goes over sheep-bitten turf,
Where the bent grass beats upon the unploughed poorland
And the pine woods roar like the surf.

Here the Roman lived on the wind-barren lonely,
Dark now and haunted by the moorland fowl;
None comes here now but the peewit only,
And moth-like death in the owl.

Beauty was here, on this beetle-droning downland;
The thought of a Caesar in the purple came
From the palace by the Tiber in the Roman townland
To this wind-swept hill with no name.

Lonely Beauty came here and was here in sadness,
Brave as a thought on the frontier of the mind,
In the camp of the wild upon the march of madness,
The bright-eyed Queen of the blind.

Now where Beauty was are the wind-withered gorses
Moaning like old men in the hill-wind's blast;
The flying sky is dark with running horses
And the night is full of the past.

And the sentry on the rampart saw the distance dying
In the smoke of distance blue and far,
And heard the curlew calling and the owl replying
As the night came cold with one star;

And thought of home beyond, over moorland, over marshes,
Over hills, over the sea, across the plains, across the pass,
By a bright sea trodden by the ships of Tarshis,
The farm, with cicadae in the grass.

And thought, as I, 'Perhaps I may be done with living
Tomorrow, when we fight. I shall see those souls no more.
O, beloved souls, be beloved in forgiving
The deeds and the words that make me sore.'

28 *22 May*

Dear Margaret, I found these in a shop here. You may have them already, for perhaps they were made early in the war, when the enemy first went back. If they were made recently, since his present retreat, they may be new to you, and you might like to have them for Edward's sake. They were the only ones I could find of Hébuterne.

They give no sort of sense of the awful romantic loneliness of that deserted town.

Like most of the French towns here, it stands in a sort of open woodland or orchard, and a good deal of it still stands, and it is a long straggling place, mostly ruin, but plainly a town; and the spring is beginning all over it but there is nobody there. You can walk across it or through it and see no one. It is like a place dead of the plague. And all the roads to it are deserted and all the towns near it are deserted, except for the wild cats, which go about singing in the moonlight till it gives one the grue.

All good wishes to you. Always yours sincerely   *John Masefield*

29 *15 June*   *Boar's Hill, Oxford*

My dear Margaret, I am so glad that you can come on Monday.

Gatti's* has 3 entrances. I will be at the one in the west Strand, nearly opposite Charing Cross station, at 1 pm.

It would be very nice if you would both lunch daily with me there during my stay, but I suppose you go roving.

We both very much hope that your mother is better now.

We all send greetings to you all.

Yours very sincerely   *John Masefield*

If you do not know it, and could go down by river-steamer, you would like Greenwich and Greenwich park.

30 *20 June*   *British Museum*

My dear Margaret, Thank you both so much for your kind thought, but tomorrow you must be my guests; and I will be yours, if you insist, at some future beano. I have planned it all for tomorrow, so please YOU are to lunch with Me. I shall have it all arranged today, so that you won't have a chance of upsetting the scheme.

I hope that you are having a good day at Boar's Hill today.
It is awfully nice of you both to spare me tomorrow.
I hope so very much that your Mother is really better.
With my greetings to her and you and to your Father.
Always sincerely yours   *John Masefield*

I hope Edward's board is being nice to him.

31   *28 June*   *Boar's Hill, Oxford*

My dear Margaret, Tucked away in this cotton wool you will find two little tiny breloques, or watch-chain amulets, one for you and one for Edward, if you will accept them.

They are bits of stone from the mound on which the windmill of Pozières used to stand, right on the top of the ridge or crest of the battlefield of the Somme. You might like to have them as curios, though I suppose few jewels have cost more than the stones of that mound, rightly considered.

We suppose that you are already gone into the green wood.
'Maid Margaret* to the wood is gon.'

Con sends her dear love to you, and all our best thoughts go to you in your new life. We hope that it will be happy and pleasant, not far from Oxford, and with lots of holidays.

All happy fortune to you. Yours ever sincerely   *John Masefield*

32   *18 July*   *Boar's Hill, Oxford*

My dear Margaret, We would not like the anniversary of our meeting you to pass without a message. We are so awfully glad that you are coming so soon to stay with us. It will be a very great pleasure to all of us.

It has been a great happiness to us to know 'the Bridges'. We hope that it will not be long before you and Edward come to celebrate the peace with us in the happy lodge of Ireland, and to talk of the first time you came, when war was declared*. All greetings to you both from Con and myself.   [unsigned]

33   *14 August*   *Boar's Hill, Oxford*

My dear Margaret, Will you accept from me these two little books, with my best wishes? They are duly written in. Inside them are two slips, also inscribed, for the two books of last week.

It was a lovely pleasure to us all to have you with us last week. We hope it may really be soon that you come again.

Poor Judith has been laid up since Saturday with a sort of a nasty bilious chill, but is now getting up and talking of sausages. She has not had any swimming since, poor child. It was kind of you to ask her to write. She was greatly pleased.

I hope that you will be posted in some nice near forest, say Bagley Wood*, and that the other lady will be a nice and friendly soul to you. All good wishes to you in your new life from all of us.

Best greetings to Edward, and congratulations on his having done with the packing.

All blessings and happy thoughts to you.

Always yours   *John Masefield*

34   *22 August*   *Boar's Hill, Oxford*

My dear Margaret, Thank you for your letter.

We saw your Mother for a few minutes on Monday evening. We thought that she was looking a little better, and happy to be settled. She even spoke of coming down to see us one day this week. She said that there was a possibility of your coming here again, before you go to your Forestry. We shall love to put you up if you will come.

The piano is with us, and your book of Beethoven on the top of it entirely deceives our visitors, who think us choice souls indeed, to play only Beethoven. Judith plays chopsticks, and Lewis picks out bits of Holy Holy Holy and God save the King, which must put us right with Mrs Graham if she ever goes by.

I am sorry that you have been kept uneasily by your Department, though you get more of Edward by it. We all hope now that we may see you here again before you start. Please know that you could not come inconveniently for us; we can always put you up. It does seem hard that you should have to wait like this when you have such lovely leggings. They are the kind I used to see on all the most august legs in France.

You will remember, won't you, that I have a very fine open-air sort of sheath knife for you, if that sort of thing will be of any use, either against robbers in the forest, or for the umbels of deer that you will probably have to live on.

This morning, I heard strange people in the house and thought it was the bread, so took no notice, as every body else was gone swimming and I was trying to do accounts. Presently I went into the garden and found four strangers wandering around. They turned out to be the Asquiths*, Mr, Mrs, Violet and a friend, and I suppose not Solomon in all his glory, nor all his wives in all their no doubt more expensive glory were arrayed like one of them. They were dressed in the morning mist caught about them with garlands of flax blossom; they floated around for some time and presently motored away and blew kisses as they went.

Neither Jude nor Lew can swim yet, but both are near it, and both are a little prickly about it.

We all send our greetings to you and Edward.

Yours always   *John Masefield*

35 *28 August*

My dear Margaret, Thank you so much for your letter. We were all awfully glad to hear that you like the life. It was very nice of you to write so soon.

The knife is going off to you in a separate registered packet. It isn't over sharp, I'm afraid, and I can't find my hone to put an edge on it, but I know you will be glad of a chance to strop it on your leggings in the proper forester style. If it is awkward, hanging from your girdle, with its rather too heavy handle, will you please let me know, and I'll try to get you a proper sailor's sheath knife, which might be handier.

We dined at the Pearces' on Saturday, and saw your Mother

and Father there; your Mother very well, we thought. Con saw her again today, coming back from Oxford; she seems really better.

The piano is fairly busy now. Lewis spends part of each day standing perilously on a chair in front of it. He opens the top and holds it open with one hand, while he strikes a note with the other hand, or with a foot, and peers in to see the jack move. Sometimes one hears Nana saying, 'Now you look in and watch, and I'll put my foot on the pedal and then come down with a Pumm.' With Pumms and Chopsticks we fleet the time pleasantly as they did in the golden age.

You now see the advantages of travel. All your life long, you will be able to say that you have seen a man who weighed 29 stone. I never have, though I did once see the famous Jolly Jumbo, a sporting publican of a jovial appearance, who weighed 28 stone; but then, Jolly J used to take carriage exercise, and no doubt kept himself fine, whereas your man takes his ease at his inn. If Jolly J had been anyways ambitious, I've no doubt he could have weighed 30 stone; but he used to scorn delights and live laborious days, driving round in a little cart to race meetings. He had a little pony, like Yankee Doodle, that used to tote him around.

Then, though I never saw her, I have seen the posters of 'Bundant Bella who was said (in the posters) to be of a matronly cut. She was an American lady, and the posters used to read
Have you seen Bundant Bella?
She's Fat.
Gee, she's Fat.
She's Awful Fat.
How do you get on with the Welsh men? Are they Welsh, or only Bordery, in Radnorshire*? Probably they have a charm at first, like most Celts, from their manners to strangers. Do they say of Lloyd George what I once heard a Welshman say of Joseph Chamberlain 'Py tam, he wass a little Jesus Christ.'

You asked me about Arthur Ransome*. He is a very nice, gentle young fellow, not a great writer, but a hard-working and pleasant kind of mind, full of interest in all kinds of life and writing, and well-read in many ways. His time in Russia may make him a little more real and a little less critical in his writing; and then, if he will write the tale of his romantic past, among publishers, he will do a fine book. I used to see him at work in an office, with a publisher at the next table. The publisher used to have a pint flask of whiskey in front of him, and this flask used to have a stopper of rolled up paper in it. From time to time, the publisher used to say O God, and then he would reach for the flask, pull out the paper stopper with his teeth, spit it out onto the table and take a swig from the flask, and then put it by till he said O God again.

After this publisher went the way indicated above, AR worked for another, who was either a quadrigamist or a trigamist, and a man of some genius. He kept all his wives in ignorance of each other for a long time. I met him once, about 1911, before the smash, and a very sinister card he was, and he foretold this war in a very strange and sinister way. He is now in prison for quadrigamy unless they have let him out.

We all send greetings to you. All happy fortune to the work.
Yours always   *John Masefield*

36   *4 September*

My dear Margaret, We were delighted to have your jolly letter this morning. Thank you so much for it. I am so happy to think that you are liking the life and cutting such a figure with the dagger. But I am a little afraid of your being sopped and soaked in the rain, and then getting chilled in the drive home and so falling ill again. What do you wear against wet? I think you ought to get a sailor's southwester (the yellow kind) as they are the best of all head-dresses in wet weather, and the ordinary sailor's yellow oilskin coat, not the long floppy black thing which reaches to the ankles, but the reefer coat made for men to go aloft in. Then with this you ought to wear what sailors used to wear but no longer do, a tarpaulin apron, which was light, a little longer than a kilt, and made either of linen oiled or of fine canvas tarred or painted. The general effect of these things, added to the knife and the leggings, would be worth your considering some Saturday night.

Judith started a letter to you some time ago, but it got torn in two by accident. She will be writing very soon though, and is very pleased at being asked.

We saw your Mother here two days ago. She is very well and says that she very much likes the cottage* in the wood. She is coming to sup with us on Sunday.

I have felt unhappy for a long time that I did not go to Boulogne to see you, when you were ill. It would have been a little difficult, but I could have done it, and wanted to, and if I had come, I could have taken you for a drive, and brought you some duck patés and chocolate truffles and things (which may well have sealed your fate), and the thought that these things may have cheered up a bad time worries me now. I did not come, because I was not sure that it would have been approved of by the canteen people or by the MO in charge of you. I think now that this was stupid; but that is how it was; and I am very sorry now that I did not come; for I ought to have, with you ill like that.

Judith has christened the two sailor's hammocks with names which give her peculiar pleasure. Mine she calls Louzy Liza and her own she calls Flea-ey Flopsie. We aren't sleeping in them these nights, as she is playing nurse to Lew, before being away; but at the end of the week we shall be back there.

It is the greatest of pities that you aren't staying here now. Scarcely has one risen from bed when Nature offers you a plum, soft, sweet, pulpy, wet and squashy on the palate, with a melting dew upon it and a colour like a sunset in fine weather. Then, while the taste is still a memory, a pear falls from the bough, oozing some luscious juice, or an apple from among the leaves reminds one, by her scarlet, of a rose, and by her fragrance of the gardens of the Hesperides. At another turn comes Pratley with grapes or Judith with a neat greengage or Lewis with a tin of blackberries. It would be lovely to feast you on these things.

You will notice the prose style of the above; it is based on Cervantes.

Walpole* may be here tomorrow to tell us about Russia; and Nevinson* comes on Saturday to mourn about something else: 'A nice funereal plume/Lends to his talk a quiet touch of gloom.'

It seems we have just invented a new gun which cannot miss. It was invented by a man who got away from Ruhleben early in 1915, and is specially good in its lighter forms for aeroplanes and anti-aircraft.

I hope that the Crickhowell* woods will be charming.

We all send greetings and messages to you and the best of good wishes. Yours ever   *John Masefield*

37

My dear Margaret, My last letter to you was rather what Judith calls 'poty', so I must try to send you a better one this time; though I expect by this time, what with living in the open air, not far from the Welsh border, you are become a terrible fellow, and think scorn of writing and the arts, and much prefer a good song over a pot at the Chequers. 'There's some sense in that,' I expect you say, 'With a quart, and a cutty pipe, and the song of old Towzes was a good old dog, a fellow, d'ye see, can bear up against the world.'

Nevinson, who was here on Sunday, told us of his old student times at Jena, where the quart bulked rather big in daily life. The students used to go to beer gardens, and they had a rule, that if any student left his big beer-mug's lid open, he had to drink a forfeit. All the other students filled their mugs and laid them in front of him in a row, and commending himself to God the poor wretch had to drink out of them till his waist-coat buttons were judged to be insufficient for their task, when somebody would say 'Hold, enough'. He said, the beer was light and good and didn't do one much harm, unless, in rash moments, people decided to get drunk on it, which took gallons to accomplish, but that it made folks rather puffy in the face. I suppose one always has to pay some price for glory. N said that in the duelling corps at Jena, every student had to fight a duel per term; and there were five students, the glory of the University, who had had their noses cut off in duels.

> A proud and happy man is Fritz
> Because his nose was cut to bits

> But Wilhelm is inclined to pout
> He only had his eye put out.

Yesterday, to our great pleasure, the Galsworthys* suddenly appeared. They have a place in Devonshire and a little flat in London, near Charing Cross Station. They have been living in Devonshire, helping to get in the harvest, and while they were there, a relative of theirs, who has visions, saw a vision, that they would run great risk of being killed if they went to London; which rather weighed upon them, for they were a little fed up with Devon and the harvest and wanted a change. However, they thought it wiser to obey the seer, so they came here and will be here for ten days, which is very jolly for us, as they are great cronies of ours. Perhaps the seer had heard about the last air-raid, which did drop a few bombs near most of the big stations, and dropped one within 70 yards of the G's flat, and blew out Shaw's windows* across the road.

Many years ago, I had to do with a number of visionaries, who were gentle, upright souls, most romantic now, in memory. They had visions about me, sometimes, (all wrong, I think, without exception) and sometimes said they saw my past incarnations, one of which, so they said, was in Venice. It was queer; for when I was a little child, I had a way of imagining all paths and roads as water, and going along them in boats; so when I went to Venice, I thought, perhaps I shall know, that I have been here before, and be able to find my old home. But there was nothing of all this. No part of that foul, dowdy, evil-smelling city of continual sewer, meant anything at all.

One of the visionaries became a Buddhist Nun and died in her nunnery in the East a little while ago. She had been married to an actor over here, who used to beat her and rob her. He stole even her workbasket, and sold it, in order to get drink.

I often think, that if I ever travel again, I shall meet most of those mystics in odd parts of the globe. I shall smell lentils frying in a back street in Mexico, and there will be one of them cooking his supper, with the Upanishads on his knee. Then on some hill-top in Burmah, someone in a loin cloth will ask me for alms, and there will be another, all thin from fasting and all shining from spiritual grace. Then, in Rome, I shall see a brown Minor Friar praying in St John Laterans, and that will be another; and perhaps a fourth will offer me a tract at Tilbury when my ship makes port again.

The swimming still goes on. J certainly swims charmingly, and can swim on her back a little.

We all send you messages and greetings and wish all happy blessings to follow your footsteps. The best of luck to you.

Always yours   *John Masefield*

38 *12 September*

My dear Margaret, We were delighted with your happy letter. Thank you so much for it.

Many years ago, I used to see the Black Mountains* in clear weather, when it was going to rain, and one of them was called the Sugar loaf, which I always thought would be a fine kind of a mountain to live near or on. If you go up the Sugar loaf ever, you will probably see the Malvern hills quite plainly, and much very lovely country, which, being wooded, you will probably soon go to work in. When you go in to that country, you shall hear some romantic tales of it.

HW* told us all about Russia*, which is plainly in a very bad way. It seems that three things may happen: 1 The Germans may reach Petrograd and force a separate peace within the next few weeks; 2 the Germans may beguile them into a separate peace, under the plan that peace is an agreeable thing, and that they would like to help the Russians to establish a stable form of government; or, thirdly, the military autocrat may arise, to hold Petrograd, re-organize the army, and keep on fighting in a desultory and not very successful manner as at present. He thinks the first thing is the most likely and the last the least.

Apparently, the soldiers are convinced, that to desert the trenches is a most noble thing, and that all soldiers who care at all for their brother man must desert, as it is their sacred duty to do so. This makes it very difficult for the Allies to appeal to the soldiers. If our officers say, 'Come, it is base to desert'; they reply, 'Bloodthirsty hounds, it is triply base not to'; and they are gone, before they have a retort ready. If we say to the peasants, 'Will you not defend your fields and homes against the Germans?' They reply, 'We do not see any Germans. There are no Germans here. We are a lot more afraid of you French and English who *are* here.' So either way, the laugh at present is with them.

Then apparently the Japs have a big army in Manchuria, and there is some fear, lest this be due to dismember Siberia.

The situation is very like the situation in the French Revolution, only events are making it move more quickly. As in France then, everybody talks of the brotherhood of man and of the beauty of having done with Kings, while the enemy is advancing into the land to put the Kings back in their place or substitute much worse ones, in the shape of German police. There is some anarchy in the cities, and uncouth beings take pot shots at people, and then there is a chance of the railways breaking down throughout the land and causing starvation in all the cities. Very few people in Russia are educated, the few who are are either pro German, or incompetent, or corrupt, so that the outlook is bad. Hardly anybody has any feeling for Russia as a State or Country or an Idea. One gets an impression of some such helpless welter as there is in *The Brothers Karamazov**.

While HW was here, your Father and Mother came in; and they came in again last tea time. Both are very well. Your Mother seems much stronger and more able to go about.

Judith asks me to enclose her letter to you. She is very much bucked at being asked to write to you.

This is a poor letter I'm afraid, this week; I'll try to make good the deficiency next time. It is jolly to think of you having so good a time in the forests.

Judith swims with a quite beautiful stroke now, and has the rudiments of a side-stroke as well.

All blessings on you, and greetings from all of us.

Always yours   *John Masefield*

---

39   *26 September*

My dear Margaret, We always said that you were a wonder, and now here you are outshining everybody and getting five shilling raises. We are so very glad and proud of your success. Well done, you.

Judith says that there is a very good stuff for fleas called Buglets, and another called Fleo. She reads advertisements rather a lot, as she is afraid of growing fat, and keeps herself posted in flesh reducers, Antipon and Sargol etc, and she comes across these things about fleas in the course of her study. Fleas never bother me much and I don't much mind them; but once we stayed in a farm in Cornwall where we could really hear their little feet as they bounded across the old oak floors to get at us. I didn't greatly care, but Con did, saying like the French Lady, 'Ce n'est pas la piqûre, c'est la promenade.' So we got a lot of Keatings and peppered the house with it. It took all the pim out of the fleas after the first day or two. They went around mopingly, with their heads down, like Yeats's ideas of the Celts. There are worse things than fleas, though.

Often on the doorsteps of ruined villages in the pleasant summer weather one sees a soldier reading his shirt tail as though it were a *Daily Mail*. There come little clicks, as though he were fixing bayonets.

We are very much ashamed; we haven't seen your Father and Mother for a week now. We were at the Pearces on Sunday, and heard that your Father had been seeing Smuts*, and that Smuts had said that the war would go on for at least another year. We have been rather tied to the house this week as it is poor J's last few days of holidays; indeed, she goes back tomorrow; and we have been trying to temper the wind to the poor lamb. She has her Browny camera now and has begun to take photographs; and this bucks her a little, and she is still rather bucked at the thought of corresponding with eminent you.

The Galsworthys are away again, as he is rehearsing a play* in Manchester; but they will probably be back again, as they get bored in the melancholy edges of Dartmoor, and they may come for a while to the Balls' cottage. If they do, we will try to arrange a meeting between your parents and them.

I am to go to America* again at about Christmas time, as there is to be an attempt to bring about good feeling between the countries. It is not exactly the easiest thing to bring about, as our acts towards America in the early days were as Boche as any thing now done in this war, and nine years of war, the sack of Washington*, the *Alabama** and other matters, do rather rise up in our faces now (when we would like to sit down at a feast) like the bloody ghost of Banquo. The war is exceedingly unpopular there, whatever our press may say. Most of them still do not realise that they have any thing to fight about. The Boche propaganda is still everywhere (and very able); the French have very little, and ours is only now beginning to be felt. They will not feel the war until they begin to have big objectives and big casualties, and that will not be for a long time. We paid very dearly for our early Boche Kings. Even the Stuarts could hardly have made a bigger mess.

It is delightful to think of you having so good a time and getting on so well; but look here my dear you have a pretty hard day and a good deal of writing to do in the course of your work, so please never feel that my letters need answering. If you should have leisure, at any time, to write, it would be lovely to hear from you, but do not feel bound to write. Writing to you anyway is partly its own reward.

We all send special messages of greeting and congratulations to you. Come to us when you can. The best of happy times to you.

Yours always *John Masefield*

40 *3 October*

My dear Margaret, We saw your Father and Mother the day after I wrote to you last week; they came in to tea with us; and then on Sunday, when Granville-Barker* was stopping with us, I went up with him, to ask your Father about the *Salisbury Antiphonal* (I think it is called) from which there is a quotation in *The Spirit of Man**. We found them (that is your Father and Mother) in the garden, and I had my first close-at-hand view of the ruins of the house*, and a sad sight it is.

Your Father and Mother are both very well indeed. I find that I mis-stated Smuts's remarks. What he really said was, that there would be fighting all through *this* winter, but not through another winter. While we were talking, Elizabeth came in from the Pearces, where she is staying. She, too, is very well, and finds living at Cambridge very pleasant. She knows Parthian and Hittite and things, and is quite fair at Mede and Elamite.

HGB and your father discoursed of church music, mostly. It seems that Edward has written some witty letter about Wells, and they are trying to get it printed in a newspaper.

Poor J is back at school in the blackest misery. We are going over to see her on Saturday, to comfort her with pears and tea. She fears that this term is 'going to be the pim of foulness and hate.' Pim is as much as to say the limit.

It seems, that the new way of dealing with the Boche machine guns is rifle fire. The guns are placed in little concrete fort-kins, each about as big as a sentry box, sunk in the ground or let into the parapet of the trench. The dodge is to plaster the trench with rifle fire so completely that even the narrow slit in each fortkin is bound to get some bullets through it.

We've been reading various books. There is a rather amusing book (by a man Douglas) called *South Wind**, full of clever talk and scandalous doings, but without much development, and then there is another rather amusing one, by a boy of 17, about life at a public school*. It is said to be Sherborne School, and the book is very good, for a boy, though I don't think he'll ever write anything else, and it isn't so complete as the book about Harrow, the Harrovians. His main point is, that the public schools are fairly rotten places, for education. However, he doesn't tell the whole truth.

Bessie, our little nurse, was in London on Sunday, and came in for an air-raid.

All good wishes and greetings from us all.

Yours ever   *John Masefield*

41   *8 October*

Dear Margaret, The last letter was very scrappy and bitty, and I hesitated to send it. I will try to make this one rather better.

We have been seeing a great many Americans (it seems) this week; so far, a very fine lot of people, mainly doctors and administrators. They say, that the first American division* has now gone into the line, somewhere in France; I should think in one of the French sectors, between, say, Toul and Verdun. The Boche have been expecting them for some time, and have been very eager to get good information about them and about those who will follow them. They have been issuing Army Orders, promising '500 francs, a fortnight's leave and the iron X' to the first Boche soldier who will bring in an American, alive or dead. I don't expect they would torture an American, or treat him worse than they treat our own men, but they have a passion for minute facts, and won't be happy till they know how many buttons an American soldier wears on his waistcoat, and whether the padres fasten their collars at the back or not

> Mit Arbeit und mit Einzelnheit
> Wir wollen Schweinhund Yankees fight.

The 1st division however will be about as full of pim as the Australians were in Gallipoli, and will welcome any Fritz who comes to win his reward.

Miss Mary King was in a shop here the other day and was

served by an old Boche, who said, 'Very nice vindy vetter. Keep avay der aeroplane raids.'

There is a story going about (perhaps I told you) of a party of American soldiers twitting a party of Australian soldiers, who, being savage from some temporary set-back, upped with their guns and shot all the Americans dead. Lady R* was convinced of its truth, and as it seemed to me to be just the kind of story which Boche agents would spread abroad in America, I took great pains to get at the truth of the matter, and have today heard from HQ that the story is utter bunkum and that nothing of the kind has ever happened at all, tho' HQ, being in a human mood, adds 'of course they will both get drunk together someday somewhere; and then there is every probability of a fight.'

We went over on Saturday to see poor J at her school, which she calls 'a dismle hole', or 'this black hole of Calcutta'. It is a fairly nice old Georgian house, with pannelled [*sic*] rooms in it, but faces north, and has great elms in front of it, so the effect is rather 'dismle'. We took her some pears and grapes and chocolate, but it was a melancholy time. School is certainly a black hole of Calcutta to send a child to. If children only had power commensurate with the wisdom of their instincts what jovial bonfires we should see.

At this point your very kind and nice letter came. Thank you so much for it, but as I said before you must not feel bound to write. We all love you very dearly and it is lovely to hear from you from you, [*sic*] but you have little time, and I will write any how every week and you needn't feel bound to reply, please. Only please send a card if the address changes. I have to thank you for a nice card as well.

It is very good of you to think of writing to Judith; she will love to have a letter from you. The address is: at Mayortorne Manor, Wendover, Bucks. We lived near Wendover some years ago, and a dismle hole it was, where after youths of drunkenness and maturities of calvinism people had old ages of lunacy. But since the war, it has had a Camp, and oh the happy change; brisk young men and smart young ladies, tremendous shops, and bands and flowers, and a pleasant taste of the new Jerusalem (i.e. Rothschild's castle up the valley).

We haven't seen your people for a week now, except Elizabeth, who has now gone back to Cambridge. We are going up to see them this afternoon.

I've not seen the Tolstoi diaries*, unless they are the reminiscences and personal jottings published some years ago. *The Times* today says that the Tolstoi property* has just been looted by the peasants on it, which is a sad ironical thing, tho' perhaps Madam Tolstoi is a little trying and brought it on herself.

We've not read anything very good lately. Wells's *Soul of a Bishop** is pretty fair till about 2 thirds through and then it goes off. There is a

II   *Boar's Hill, Oxford*

This is the second sheet. I find my pad is at an end, and cannot find another so have to use this sheet.

Mrs Dowdall here, friend to the Raleighs*. She writes neat malicious books and one of them called *The Kaleidoscope** is pretty fair. Would you like to have it sent to you? We have Sorley's poems,* too, and Vernède's* as well, and the posthumous Swinburne* poems. If you like, I will send you these all together. The new Galsworthy book, *Beyond,** is not bad, and as Judith says, 'I like it where the husband gets drunk.' All these are at your service and it will be a pleasure to send them if they will be a pleasure to you.

It is very sad. 'Gay Robin is now no more.' Nothing in his life became him like his leaving of it, and we are going to buy 2 new pigs in his stead.

We love to think of you having a happy time. We were thinking and saying only 2 days ago what a world of difference you had made to all our lives and what a joy it has been to know you.

All blessings on you my dear. Yours ever   *John Masefield*
Bobby Phillimore is now markedly better, so Lion says.

42   *10 October*   *Boar's Hill, Oxford*

My dear Margaret, I sent you a letter the other day addressed to your villa at Talgarth.* Perhaps this was wrong, and it may never have reached you. This goes to Crickhowell P O and if you get this and not the other you will be able to think of what you have missed.

Your Mother came to see us yesterday and seemed very well and bright, only she says that she does not yet feel up to going out

Margaret Bridges

in the evenings. Your Father is re-pointing* the Psalms, which is certainly a righteous task, acceptable to God and Man.

Jude, who does not take altogether to righteous tasks, abstains from church on Sunday, so last Sunday, finding the church time a little dull, she knotted up an acquaintance's pyjamas into lusty tough knots; and had a great reward at bedtime, when the person (a great friend of yours) tried to go to bed.

We want to know, please, if it would be any good, sending you some pears? Probably all Welsh pears are stolen while still green, and it would be nice to send you some when ours ripen a little.

All greetings and messages from all of us.

Yours ever   *John Masefield*

Dear Margaret, Looking over the pears in the loft, I find none quite fit to send, though a good many are coming on and will be ready soon, so perhaps next week, if you will send your new address, we may have some for you.

I have been in London this week, and so missed seeing your Mother, who was in here on Monday: very well, I think, as she was when I saw her last week, but not able to do very much. We are to dine there tomorrow evening.

I didn't hear any gossip in London, as all my people were out, but I saw some very good war photographs, and I saw the guards doing all sorts of Prussian clicks in the Buckingham drillground. It was a most Boche-y sight. They pranced with their knees just as though William* were there. Later on, I met Gosse* in the London Library. He said, he had given Asquith* an autumn dinner every year for 18 years and had introduced him to over 100 scientists and men of letters.

> Were there a hundred such as Gosse
> A's butcher would sustain a loss
> And not a scientist could say
> He hadn't been introduced to A.

Harley* says he has a glorious anti-submarine suit that he will lend me to go to America in. You put it on over your pyjamas when you go to bed, and then if you are torpedoed, up you hop, and put the tube in your mouth and puff yourself up, like your bicycle tyre that I mended for you (with your help) and then when the ship sinks and the dying groans ring in your ears you say 'Look at me, how calm I am,' for you just float about, quite warm and unsinkable; and you pull out your bully beef from your pocket and eat a neat lunch, to the admiration of the gulls. This, of course is the theory; the practice may be a different matter.

Your Mother shewed us an excellent photograph of you in your leggings, with drawn knife. Will you not please very kindly let us have a print of the photograph, for we only have the little pass-port one of you which isn't very like?

Robin, who is dead, is a lovely pig, and we are living on him, and we are all so fat and shiny.

We hear that you are now in command of your section and should be called Captain Margaret.

I hope that you had a good time in Swansea with Edward. Sailors many years ago used to rank Swansea pretty low, as about the limit, even for a seaport. I hope it is not too black a place for a convalescent home. Cardiff, its sweet sister, must be fairly near you. One should go to these places once, just to see them.

All greetings from us and congratulations on your promotion. Yours ever   *John Masefield*

44   *23 October*

My dear Margaret, Thank you very much for your letter.

The pears have gone off in a basket, and should have reached you by this time unless lifted by the Welsh on the way. I hope they will cheer a lunch or two in some lovely forest; but they do not travel over well. You shall have *Beyond* when we have your new address. Edward is said to be here now, having arrived last night, but we have not seen him yet; I suppose he is sleeping in the library, and we cannot help feeling that he ought to be with us.

There were rumours (of the usual war kind) that the last batch of Zepps came to within 6 miles of Oxford. The lights went out in Oxford, as an alarm was given, but the present rumour is that the Zepps were really making for Didcot and missed their way and had to return. I think they found the Thames and followed it up as far as they could see it.

We met a man in the Trade Intelligence last Sunday. He said that the Boche have enough food but are really suffering from a want of wool, which is so scarce that no man can buy wool of any kind without giving back an equal weight of old or worn wool. Then they have set to work to make a kind of a synthetic wool, or a wool-equivalent, out of wood pulp or bark fibre, and have made a very good one, but so costly that none but the rich can afford it. We, too, have been making this stuff, and ours is better than the Boche and quite cheap. Then, the Boche complaint, that our blockade robs the Boche child of his dear little milk and cream, and his nice little mug of a morning, is due to the Boche habit of using every drop of milk and cream in his explosives factories. You get a beastly kind of oil out of cream, it seems, which the Boche use a lot of.

We've been reading a horrid book about the Boche, called *Salt and Savour**, all about a nice English girl who marries a horrid Boche captain and has the devil of a time. She had much better have gone to live in Swansea, and then she would have had a lovely time going to the cinema with her own countrymen, tho it is true she wouldn't have seen Berlin. Mr and Mrs Warren were here yesterday and Mr W has just come back from Corfu, where he was right alongside Wilhelm's palace, which he says is simply the limit of vulgar display, with awful statues everywhere, Kultur enlightening the world, Bismarck awakening the Boche World-Soul, Moltke handing the torch of Efficiency to Hindenburg, Arminius laying the foundation stone of the Kolossos etc. Then old Wilhelm is about the limit with the Corfu villages. He orders them to put out their lights at ½ past 8 each night, and forbids them to have dogs or cocks or any noisy beast of that sort, which is pretty cool, even if his sister did marry Tino*. When he heard that the French had turned his palace into a hospital, he swore that he would send the Austrian fleet down to blow it all to pieces, but so far this hasn't come off.

24 Oct. I had to stop at this point yesterday for Edward came in to see us, with your Mother, both extraordinarily well we thought. It was a great pleasure to us to see Edward, and he was awfully happy to be back at home. They told us that it was your Father's birthday so in the evening we took him up some grapes (some small un-Judithed bunches) as a birthday present, and we did just see him in the dark.

I am so sorry about *Beyond*. It seems that Con has just lent it to Mrs Pearce, so that it may be some days before I can send it. I'm so sorry. Is there anything else you would care for? We have Wells's *God and I**, or whatever it is called, and his *Research Magnificent** and his *Passionate Friends** (they aren't very passionate, for Wells), but all 3 books are pretty feeble. A publisher sent me a book called *The Oilskin Packet**, which (he said) was better than *Treasure Island*, but mon Dieu, I fiche myself of it, it is a kind of a boy's book, full of folly.

The American mail takes longer and longer now. I have had some letters this week which were posted in New York 26 days before. I rather think they must come with the transports by way of Bordeaux now.

Edward gave us a cheery account of you. I am so glad you like the work and are having a good time. I hope that I may be here when you get your leave.

With love from all of us, Yours ever   *John Masefield*

By the way, our man said, that the Boche use fur a great deal now, instead of wool. They go to fetch a rabbit skin to wrap the baby Boches in. When they are all in skins, they will be just about fittingly clad for such a warrior people. I think they wore dirty skins in Tacitus, whereas we nice Britons simply heightened our natural good points with a little woad.

The Blacksmith

The blacksmith in his sparky forge
Beat on the white-hot softness there;
Even as he beat he sang an air
To keep the sparks out of his gorge.

So many shoes the blacksmith beat,
So many shares and links for traces,
So many builders' struts and braces,
Such tackling for the chain-fore-sheet,

That, in his pride, big words he spake;
'I am the master of my trade,
What iron is good for I have made,
I make what is in iron to make.'

Daily he sang thus by his fire,
Till one day, as he poised his stroke
Above his bar, the iron spoke,
'You boaster, drop your hammer, liar.'

The hammer dropped out of his hand,
The iron rose, it gathered shape,
It took the blacksmith by the nape,
It pressed him to the furnace, and

Heaped fire upon him till his form
Was molten, flinging sparks aloft,
Until his bones were melted soft,
His hairs crisped in a fiery storm.

The iron drew him from the blaze
To place him on the anvil, then
It beat him from the shape of men,
Like drugs the apothecary brays;

Beat him to ploughing-coulters, beat
Body and blood to links of chain,
With endless hammerings of pain,
Unending torment of white heat;

And did not stop the work, but still
Beat on him while the furnace roared;
The blacksmith suffered and implored,
With iron bonds upon his will.

And, though he could not die nor shrink,
He felt his being beat by force
To horse shoes stamped on by the horse,
And into troughs whence cattle drink.

He felt his blood, his dear delight,
Beat into shares, he felt it rive
The green earth red; he was alive,
Dragged through the earth by horses' might.

He felt his brain, that once had planned
His daily life, changed to a chain
Which curbed a sail or dragged a wain,
Or hoisted ship-loads to the land.

He felt his heart, that once had thrilled
With love of wife and little ones,
Cut out and mingled with his bones
To pin the bricks where men rebuilt.

He felt his very self impelled
To common uses, till he cried,
'There's more within me than is tried,
More than you ever think to weld.

For all my pain I am only used
To make the props for daily labour;
I burn, I am beaten like a tabor
To make men tools; I am abused.

Deep in the white heat where I gasp
I see the unmastered finer powers,
Iron by cunning wrought to flowers,
File-worked, not tortured by the rasp.

Deep in this fire-tortured mind
Thought bends the bar in subtler ways,
It glows into the mass, its rays
Purge, till the iron is refined.

Then, as the full moon draws the tide
Out of the vague uncaptained sea,
Some moon power there ought to be
To work on ore; it should be tried.

By this fierce fire in which I ache
I see new fires not yet begun,
A blacksmith smithying with the sun,
At unmade things man ought to make.

Life is not fire and blows, but thought,
Attention kindling into joy,
Those who make nothing new destroy,
O me, what evil I have wrought.

'O me,' and as he moaned he saw
His iron master shake, he felt
No blow, nor did the fire melt
His flesh, he was released from law.

He sat upon the anvil top
Dazed, as the iron was dazed, he took
Strength, seeing that the iron shook,
He said, 'This cruel time must stop.'

He seized the iron and held him fast
With pincers, in the midmost blaze,
A million sparks went million ways,
The cowhorn handle plied the blast.

'Burn, then,' he cried; the fire was white,
The iron was whiter than the fire.
The fireblast made the embers twire,
The blacksmith's arm began to smite.

First vengeance for old pain, and then
Beginning hope of better things,
Then swordblades for the sides of Kings
And corselets for the breasts of men.

And crowns and such like joys and gems.
And stars of honour for the pure,
Jewel of honour to endure,
Beautiful women's diadems.

And coulters, sevenfold-twinned, to rend,
And girders to uphold the tower,
Harness for unimagined power,
New ships to make the billows bend,

And stores of fire-compelling things
By which men dominate and pierce
The iron-imprisoned universe
Where angels lie with banded wings.

45 *2 November*   *Boar's Hill, Oxford*

My dear Margaret, So many thanks for your letter and for
sending back the pear basket.

I am late with my letter this week, as I put off writing, thinking
that we should be seeing your Father and Mother either last night
or the night before, and so be able to send you news of them; but
the weather has been bad, and we have been rather tied to the
house by Lewis, since Bessie* has gone away to be married, and
so we haven't been able to see your people and can send you no
news of them at all.

Bessie comes back next week, for her poor man is in the army
and only gets 6 days, and I don't know when she will see him
again.

There is a general gloom about Italy*, but I do not see that it is
so terrible. The Boche are probably counting in as prisoner, every
wounded and killed man, or bit of man, on the field, and I do not
doubt that many of their 'captured guns' are rifles. Still, it has
been a nasty knock. I think that it is a sign that Austria is on her

very last legs, and if it should fail to take Italy out of the war, then
the Boche will find themselves committed to a great expenditure
of men and guns on a front which will not be the decisive front. It
is just 3 months ago that I heard that Lloydie* was keen on having
a go at Austria from the Italian front, putting in ½ a million men
there and trying to reach Vienna. Now I suppose they'll have to
try something of the kind.

You shall have Beyond as soon as we get it back from Mrs
Pearce. My American publisher has just sent me Upton Sinclair's
book* about coal-mining (as dismal a scene of horror as meat-
curing in his Chicago book*). It will make you jolly glad you aren't
a coal-miner, for it seems that you don't have bull-dogs and
prize-fights, nor racing whippets, if you are a coal-miner in the
US. You get a grim time, and then the sack, if you aren't blown up
first. I've also got '3 plays* for a negro theatre' which may be
rather fun.

We are reading C. Mackenzie* here, for the first time. It is very
prettily done, but so far we don't find that his things are alive
much. Perhaps in the years before the war people who wrote
were too fond of subordinating the souls they wrote about to the
comfort and beauty of their surroundings and their tastes; and C
M seems to be quite as keen about his people's furniture and
books and gardens as about their actions under the harrow of life.

We hope that you are still having a jolly time. I expect you are
so hungry that like Keats in Scotland* 'a ham goes but a very little
way'. Do you still get any sing songs on Saturdays?

We all send you our greetings. Best wishes to you.

Yours ever sincerely   *John Masefield*

46   *3 November*   *Boar's Hill, Oxford*

Dear Margaret, Thank you for your card, telling me of your
change of address. I am sorry to say, that I sent a letter to you at
Brecon*, only last night; however I hope that it may reach you; for
perhaps the lady's legs won't swell with redirecting a letter.

I hope that the new place will be agreeable. You will be able
soon to write a neat book, Picturesque Wales, or from Usk* to
Towy*, and make much more than I can say, from the advertisements of the hotels alone. L George would make you a Dame at

once, as well. You would be frightfully bricked to be a Dame, and look how proud we should be.

    Yours always sincerely   *John Masefield*

47 [*undated*]

My dear Margaret, Thank you so much for your nice letter. It is splendid to think that you will so soon be here again. I shall be in civvies when you come, so your gaiters will hold undisputed sway, unless Judith can contrive some counter-swank.

    Things do not seem very rosy, here and abroad. A friend came to us from Paris on Sunday, where he had been seeing a certain person, who said, that his great fear for the last months had been a defection of Switzerland, who, under pressure and intrigue, was suspected, of being about to let the enemy through into France. However, quite recently, this fear has been rather lessened, and the theory has been, that it was only a rumour put abroad by enemy agents to weaken the French moral, already shaken, perhaps, by the Russian collapse. Our friend said, that financially we were all right and could go on for years, but that there would be the most appalling famine ever known, in Russia, in the spring, and that under the pressure of that famine Russia might cease even to be a country. He said, that with the need of using ships to convey food to Europe, the American armies would hardly start for France in force, till 1918, autumn, or 1919, winter. The question comes, will France and Italy be able to hold out so long?

    We rather think, that the peace party will split the Government before very long, and bring the question of peace into party politics.

    We have been seeing your parents several times during the last ten days; both are well; and your Mother seems to have quite recovered from her cold.

    Murray came up yesterday, with a tale of an old wise incredibly learned Jew prophet, who prophesies correctly about the war (he must be a fairly rare kind of a prophet). This man's latest prophecy, is, that a sort of pestilence of anarchy will burst out in Russia, and spread westward over Germany, break Germany, and then spread westward to France and ourselves. This is not to happen at once, but be the result of and reaction from too much military discipline.

Dorothy Warren was here, too. She has cut her hair and looks like the portrait of a young man by Botticelli. She says that Peter is pretty happy in his prison camp.

Somewhere in Wales you can see a Roman gold mine with all the ore-crushers and washers just as the Romans left them. This would be better worth the PM's eye than a lead mine and it wouldn't get nice you into a row for chopping your pit props wrong.

We all send love and greetings to you. I'm sorry my last notes were such poor scraps, but I wanted to send you some word and couldn't manage more, not having time. The rats tails tremble in anticipation of your holiday. All blessings on you, my dear Margaret, from all our household, who all long to see you.

Yours ever   J.M.

48   *6 November*   *Boar's Hill, Oxford*

My dear Margaret, Tomorrow I hope to send you Galsworthy's novel, *Beyond*. I hope that it will not be a nuisance to you to have it now.

We have seen your Father and Mother; we went up there on Sunday night and found them both very well indeed. Your father has been doing a couplet* for a memorial (which I hope will some day be put up at Gheluvelt) to the Worcester battalion which saved the line in Oct 1914. I thought the couplet very splendid. I hope that I betray no confidence in talking of it.

I've read your Conrad book of *Victory**, and though it didn't take me by storm, it struck me as a big piece of symbol, and rather haunting. The people impress me more as spirits than as people.

We all send you our love and wish that you were here again.

All blessings on you. Yours ever sincerely   *John Masefield*

49   *13 November*

My dear Margaret, It was a very delightful pleasure to have your charming long letter this morning. Thank you so much for it. We are so glad that you are having a good time. We long to see you again and to hear all about hell-fire.

We've been reading a little play for a Negro Theatre, which is partly about hell-fire, and it just misses being terrific; and you would enjoy reading it, it is quite unlike anything else. As soon as I hear that you are in any sort of settled address I will send it to you. It will only take 10 minutes to read.

Do you go to services in Welsh and hear preaching in Welsh? I used to hear a Welsh clergyman in London who used to preach to an old Welsh soldier who couldn't go to church, and they used to coo at each other when they got excited, and then they would shed tears, and then the old soldier would curse his wife for not having dinner ready and say D— her, he knew she was trying to poison him, but he had told the doctors to cut him up when he died, so that, D—her, the poison would be discovered.

The suicide pool must be a little like the ponds in China, where they have to put up notices: 'Daughters must not be drowned here. By Order.'

The Italian business* is very bad indeed and may not be at its worst yet. It is a great score for William, just when he wanted it most, and it must have been most excellently done by the Boche staff. How we shall crow when we do something like it. The worst of it is, that with all the Italian guns gone, the line may be untenable anywhere.

The late PM* was here on Sunday, and Con said, that she hoped that he would soon be back in the PM ship, and he beamed all over his face, and said 'my dear lady, it isn't such fun being PM in these days.' He told us that Kerensky* had been a great ass, living in guilty splendour in the late Czar's own bedroom, and insisting on much such a life as the Czars had used to have; so that at last the people had rebelled. He was (the late PM) very cheerful, and indeed, to be out of the turmoil, and to see one's opponent making an ass of himself, must be not unpleasant. Mrs G. Barker came over, too, and just by the mercy of God we had not her recently divorced husband staying with us, which would have been an awkward meeting.

There is just a chance that I shall be here for Christmas, so I shall hope to see you before I go. Will you be with us, or in the cottage?

I was talking with a man about the American propaganda yesterday. He thought that we had done next to nothing there in that way, while the enemy had been doing it ever since the Boer War, and yet, whenever the Boche really got opinion on their side, they would do something silly, and upset the work of months by one clumsy and dirty crime. He said that the Boche would start some rousing lie about us, such as saying that we forbade the importation of Red X stores into Belgium, so that sick Belgians died like flies, while our brutal officials insulted kind American ladies who wanted to get the stores through. This lie would come to press, and people would telephone to our officials, to ask, if it were true. We would reply, 'We are dealing with the matter,' and about a fortnight later, when the tale had been read and believed by millions, we would send out a curt official denial which nobody would bother to print.

The Mackenzie books* we've been reading are *Sinister St*, part I, *Guy and Pauline*, and *Carnival*. He is a little like the boy in *Sinister Street*, very delicate and sensitive and a little morbid, and he never seems to grow up even into a big boy, let alone a man, tho' he writes very well, (in the manner of before the war). As for the Galsworthy, you hit it off very well, in your wise way. Like Judith, 'I like it where he gets drunk,' but otherwise I don't see Fiorsen, worth a cent.

We have seen your Father and Mother: both very well indeed; and you may be seeing them next Saturday. I hope that you will have fine weather for the jaunt to them.

There is a great scheme here, for a little theatre*, to play repertory in Oxford, 'after the war'. I'll tell you about it in my next letter.

All happy fortune be about you my dear Margaret. We all send special messages of greetings to you and Edward. It will be nice for you to have one Sunday away from the theologians.

Always yours sincerely   *John Masefield*

50   *21 November*

My dear Margaret, Thank you for your card, and welcome to your new home. I hope that you will find A a pleasant billet, with lovely movies and other joys.

As far as I can make out, A is a seaside resort. I once had a nurse who had a mug, and on the mug, 'in letters all of gold,' was the inscription: 'A present from Aberystwith'*. This makes it almost certain that A is on the sea; not quite certain though, for she had a beastly little nephew, who had another mug, which had the inscription: 'A present from Llandrindod Wells'*; and it is possible, that, if the Wells, which seem to be inland, should have mugs of presentation, the having of mugs is not an infallible sign, that a place is on the sea. Perhaps they have them at all extraordinary places; so we will conclude that A is an extraordinary place. I hope you'll have a good time there.

We have been hearing a good deal about one thing and another lately; firstly, that the Boche submarines depend for their successes not on any luck, or folly of our own men, but solely on a rather rare professional skill in their commanders. It depends on their use of a few vital seconds, during which the submarine has a chance of hitting. It seems, that this skill is not common, but that it is very great in a few men, and these few clever men cause nearly all our losses. We know the names of these few men and where they live and what they look like. We know their terms of duty and when they go off duty and when they come on. When the losses on a sector begin to go up, people say, 'Here is Wilhelm, or Fritz, or Hans on duty again.'

We are getting submarines fairly well (I believe not nearly so well as Lloydie says) but we are getting them. It is thought that just at the moment all the boats have been withdrawn from commerce – attacking in order to have a big go at the American transports, or else a fleet attack on us. I expect that they may be having a big go on the Salonika force, to keep the Turks and Bulgars busy, and make them pull their pound. If all the boats were to concentrate there, while all the eastern armies had a go at our Salonika front, they might have quite a success.

The submarine crews still volunteer freely for service, in Germany. It is the only fully-fed service now in Germany, and this must be an attraction, tho' one may conclude that the percentage of loss is not very high yet.

It is said that Turkey is eager for peace at any price, but cannot find a spokesman. The land is under the thumb of these devils of the 'Union and Progress'*, and any one who speaks of peace has his throat cut.

I daresay I shall be here for Xmas Day, so I may just see you.

Bless you my dear Margaret. We all send you love and greetings. Yours ever   *John Masefield*

My dear Margaret, So many thanks for your nice letter.

I shall be sailing somewhere about a month from today, so that there will be a chance of seeing you. Mind you keep to your plan and come here a lot.

About short comedies: Galsworthy's *Little Man** is very funny, but has 3 or 4 male parts. Granville-Barker's *Rococo** is very funny; in what is called a 'Knock about' way, i.e., the people knock each other about, but it needs about 3 men. Yeats's *Pot of Broth** is a brilliant little farce, and has 2 men's parts, and I was once much amused by a play called (I think) *The Bishop and the Burglar*, which also needed 2 men. The Bishop catches the Burglar and tries to make the Burglar marry his daughter, who is a pious lady. 'Gawd, guvnor,' says the Burglar, 'I'll reform rather.' It's not very refined but awfully funny. Then Barrie's, '*12 pound look'**, 1 male part, is very good, and so is Miss Symonds's *Feed the Brute**, which has also 1 man in it. I don't know who publish these. Stanley Houghton* wrote some 1 act plays, published by Sidgwick and Jackson, but I do not know these. I used to have a translation of a screamingly funny Spanish farce called *Love's a Dream*, but this is in store in London and I can't get at it. These are all that I can think of at the moment. Barrie has written a lot of 1 act plays, all pretty good. All good wishes to your dramatic entertainment anyhow. I hope that the movies came up to sample.

We saw your Mother on Sunday: she seems really better.

Love from all of us. Yours ever sincerely   *John Masefield*

I send this hurried scrap to tell you about the few plays.

52 *24 January*   *at the Harvard Club, 27 West 44th St, New York*

My dear Margaret, I am writing this in the train somewhere not far from New York, and I wish I were in New York for then I could come by some breakfast, which I sadly need, a throat lozenge being a rotten substitute.

I wonder where you are now and what you are doing. I suppose you covered yourself with glory in your play and are now in rehearsal of another.

I had a dismal journey across. Every time, I repeat to myself the ballad 'O never more do I intend/For to cross the raging main' but this time it was the limit. We ran at once into heavy weather, much wind and an evil sea, and though I am used to being sick, I plumbed unknown depths this time. One has to wear that beastly patent waistcoat all the time, and it has a penetrating reek of rubber tyre solution, and whiffs of this were about me day and night.

Now that I am here, it isn't so bad, though it is pretty cold, and with the snow and the cold the trains are late. This one is an hour and a half late already, and I can't get any breakfast till she gets in. But joy, oh joy, my dear Margaret, I see the pinnacles of NY ahead. You will think it a poor compliment, that I should be thinking of breakfast while I write to you; but it is only the baser and earthy self of me that thinks of breakfast; the rest of me scorns such things and is calm and breathes a purer air.

America at war is quite unlike any America known to me. It is, here, in the East, strongly pro-War, but even here the old Boche god of the weather fights against us. The winter has been terrific ever since November, and the harbours have been frozen up with ice a foot thick, and it has been impossible to get coal to the consumers. All things have been delayed and held up by the frost, and there has been a lot of suffering among the poor.

It is very pleasant to find England popular here, and forgiven, and admired, and made much of. I hope that our relations will not again change, but remain as they are; different indeed from what they used to be.

This is the 3rd time I have had a go at this letter today. I write this in another train, going to a place called Bridgeport, where I am to speak and (please God) sleep in a bed, instead of in a sleeper. I sleep and speak in a different place every night, and could write a noble book about the ways of travel here. How Providence watches over sinners, my dear Margaret. Yesterday I was given a set of Emerson, whom I loathe, and another friend gave me a box of ginger, which I hate, and now the beastly ginger has broken and leaked all over the Emerson, so that I needn't bother any more about either.

I do like Americans and America, but the climate is like champagne and it makes one feverish with energy.

All greetings to you, and blessings on you and your work.
Yours ever sincerely   *John Masefield*

53   *9 February*   *at 2970 Ellis Avenue, Chicago, Ill.*

My dear Margaret, Thank you so very much my dear for your kind nice letter. It was a great delight to me to get it here after speaking this morning, and I do think it was jolly good and kind and nice of you to think of writing to me and I love you for it.

I ought to have written to you more than my poor miserly once, but it has been a crowded and feverish time, with speaking once a day, sometimes twice, and many interviewers and reporters, and beastly lunches and teas where I have to say a few words, and then off to a hot train for 3 or 400 miles to repeat the process. I'll hope to write more regularly after I leave this Middle West, as it should then be less feverish.

The main thing here is the severity of the winter, which has been beyond the memory of man, with frost and heavy snow, for weeks together. This has blocked the railways, stopped all sorts of war-work, such as ship building, and made a coal-famine everywhere. Many houses have been made uninhabitable by the cold (40 or 50 degrees of frost for 8 weeks) and there has been much hardship. The trains are disorganized, and run very late (I was ten hours late on Tuesday and 4½ hours late on Wednesday) and the harbours have been frozen. People's noses and ears and fingers become very brittle in these temperatures and crack off like twigs, and many a good ear litters the pavements and it is very dangerous to blow one's nose.

I am writing this in Chicago, looking out on a grim street and the grim Lake Michigan frozen in all its waves. The street has a narrow cart track down its middle, and everywhere else great ramparts of snow from 5 to 8 feet high, rather like the parapets of trenches, and of a grey black colour, for we burn a soft coal here and there is a sort of thaw. The town is of a grey black colour in itself, and this tones off into the snow rather neatly, and the sun is shining and there are a lot of gulls picking garbage down by the lake. They are big gulls — as big as gannets, and very noble-looking.

It is said to be dangerous to flaunt one's wealth in this town. I was at a dinner the other night at which all the guests, male and female, had been robbed at one time or another, by armed bandits, all except one man, who said, 'they didn't rob me, they only hit me over the head so that I bled out of the ears, but they didn't get me down so that they could rob me.'

I hope you aren't finding the forest life too rough and hard. I hope you will go to see Con if you have an Easter holiday. All greetings and blessings and good fortunes to you.

Yours ever   *John Masefield*

54   *13 February*   *Chicago*

My dear Margaret, I am still here, speaking to city audiences of varying sizes, and being mis-reported by journalists who do not know their job. I've been described as a red revolutionary, and as a believer in brute force, and as a pacifist, and I have now grown weary of denying, but let them say what they will.

It is a great pity, but I shall miss the famous Billy Sunday* here. He is going to have a revival here next month, and is building a huge wooden shed for it, to hold 15,000 people, and according to my friend, 'There'll be some hot halleluias going around when he starts going.' I shall be away by that time, down in the south or in the west.

I met a man the other day who had been all the summer in Alaska with some Indians, and had met one Indian who used to raise the Devil. He asked this Indian if it were true that he could raise the devil, and the man said; 'Yes; bring him right here into the room.' My friend said 'Aren't you afraid of him?' and the man said, 'No, he's afraid of me, and does just what I tell him.' My friend asked, 'Well, what does the Devil look like, any way?' The Indian thought a while and said 'He looks pretty good.'

Not long ago, I was speaking in Baltimore, and a man came up to me, and said, 'Will you let me introduce myself? I'm Edgar Allan Poe.' So I looked at this man, as I thought he was pulling my leg, and I said, 'Are you sure you aren't Robert Browning?' The worst of it was I found out later that he really was called Edgar Allan Poe, being some sort of a distant relation.

I've been reading MacKail's *Life** of William Morris here. Perhaps, you never had a pre-Raphaelite period. It was a long and romantic wave with me, and out here, in this filthy flat thawing city, to read of it brings it all back, with a longing for all that Cotswold England where WM lived towards the end.

Golly, one does get homesick on these trips, and I am still only outward bound. What one wants is the little, simple quiet England of before the war, and the flowers as they were at Lollingdon, when I went there in the spring, in April, 1914.

I hope that you are having an easier time now, not bothered by the Portuguese, and finding it easier to draw rations.

Greetings to you . . . Yours ever sincerely   *John Masefield*

55   *18 February*   *Hotel Fontenelle, Omaha, Neb.*

My dear Margaret, I am writing this in this great barrack of a place, 'built,' as they say, 'for me to enjoy,' but where I shall have to be speaking to a big audience in about 20 minutes' time, so that my enjoyment is tempered.

From this place one commands a vast view of cornland, which reaches for hundreds of miles in all directions, in a prospect of fertility which makes one gasp at the power and wealth of the earth. In many places you see cornfields to the horizon on both sides of you, and the ground is so fertile that it needs no manure, and the farmers will not even go to the trouble of taking the manure from the cavalry camps. This land could feed 200 million people easily, and with intensive cultivation it could feed 3 times as many.

This is only a note. I'll try to write you a proper letter soon, and if I fail, I will write you another note.

All blessings and greetings and good wishes to you.

Yours always sincerely   *John Masefield*

56   *24 February*   *In St Louis, Mo.*

Dear Margaret, This is the noisiest town I was ever in, and about the 7th or 8th for smoke, and the 2nd for evil journalists; but it is not a bad place, and seems full of sweet musicians.

Mo. is short for Missouri, which is the Indian way of saying Dirty Water, the river here being all of that. At present, the river is full of floating ice which is arranged in huge round tables, slowly revolving and grinding off their edges.

In the summer, I can imagine nothing lovelier than to float down such a river on a raft, like Huckleberry Finn.

I may have told you, how the other day I went down into the wilds of Missouri, through the woodland, still uncleared and unsettled? I passed little lonely shacks and huts, in clearings made by burnings, where a few gipsy-looking people lived with a cow and a pig or two. In one place, there were 3 or 4 such huts together, with the notice:

The Finest Place on Earth.

Good Schools, Good Water and Good Health.

Come and live with us.

The country seemed savage for want of men, and there were lonely stagnant rivers and swamps, and a wilderness of wood, sometimes all heaped about by some old cyclone of 50 years ago, and every now and again an eagle cruizing, or a man chewing tobacco in a kind of trance, much as you or I would be if we were chewing manna.

There are 2 children here whom I have asked out to tea, and I asked them to tell me what they would specially like to have for tea. The boy said chocolate, but the girl blushed, and havered, and at last said 'Well, I don't care what people say of me. I do love a ham sandwich; I can't help it.'

I go tomorrow down into the wilderness on my way to Texas, where the bad men used to live, in the old days of the open ranges.

Barbed wire has pretty much reduced them to terms, and the state is fairly quiet now, and the old days of the cowboy are over. They used to drive vast herds of cattle every year from the Mexican frontier to the heart of Montana, and a pretty tough variety of man was the result. He used to sing the song quoted in *The Spirit of Man**, the one beginning:

> O, I am going home,
> Cow-punching for to spurn;
> I ain't got a cent, and
> I don't give a durn.

If you ever get a chance, you should read Mr Andy Adams's book, *The Log of a Cowboy**, which describes the life quite wonderfully.

I hope that you are now in some pleasant place, such as Savernake or Epping, away from Portuguese and Welsh. I suppose you have been promoted again by this time. They could not do better.

I hope that you have Edward now and then for week-ends.

All good wishes and greetings to you. All pleasant fortune attend you.

Always yours sincerely   *John Masefield*

57   *4 March*   *Georgetown, Texas*

Dear Margaret, I think I last wrote to you from St Louis, which is about 900 miles from here. Now I am out of the cold in the heat of a Texan spring, sitting on a log in the sun, and wishing I were dressed only in blue cotton overalls like the negroes.

The wind blows up from the Gulf of Mexico, about 100 miles away, and it takes all the pim out of people; one longs to lie down somewhere where one won't have to hold on, while a negro keeps away the flies.

The Spaniards were here once, and have left their mark on the towns, and there is a good deal of Spanish spoken here, and some of the shops have signs in Spanish. I hope that the siesta will still be practised here. The siesta is a jolly good idea so near the Mexican Gulf.

There are a lot of sort of cowboy ponies tethered in the town, and from time to time a man mounts one, and comes loping by,

exactly as though he were a part of the horse. The man shies
when the horse shies and sidles when the horse sidles, and when
the horse is wicked and shews his devilry the man shews something of it, too. Then the horses get something from the men.
They stand at street corners, and chew tobacco, and spit, exactly
like the men, and they have a wicked air of taking it all in and
debating what line of devilry they shall take upon it.

There are many great camps not far from here, and in one of
them is 'Guvvy' Hoffman, who was at Magdalen, and used to
come over to Lollingdon with Peter Warren and Dorothy.

Forgive a short note this time. The Gulf is hard to fight against.

All greetings to you. Always yours sincerely   *John Masefield*

58   *7 March*   *The St Anthony, San Antonio, Texas*

Dear Margaret, I wrote you a scrappy note from Georgetown the
other day, while the souther was blowing. Now I can write you
another note while the norther is blowing. When the souther
blows it is like mid July, and when the norther blows it is like early
March.

I motored down here from Georgetown, in the souther, and it
was a very lovely journey, across an Italian-looking landscape,
parched by the drought, but with some exquisite clear rivers here
and there, and a hairy parasite, known as Spanish moss, like the
scalps of 1000s of Absaloms, dangling from the trees.

As we came along, I began to notice placards at intervals; quite
small placards, written in red, beginning casually and quietly
with the statement:

Jennings!

and then beginning a catechism, which continued at intervals of
50 yards, something as follows:

Do you know Jennings?
Have you heard of Jennings?
Jennings the Drug Store
Have you met Jennings?
Jennings for Ice Cream Soda
Jennings for Cold Drinks
You may have your Thermos filled at Jennings
It is cooler in Jennings

Go to see Jennings
Talk to Jennings
Ladies Wanted at Jennings
To eat Ice Cream and Candy
Matrimonial Station at Jennings
You take your girl to Jennings
Woo her at Jennings
She will have you at Jennings
You will win her at Jennings
You can marry her from Jennings
The Soul Kiss is dead sure at Jennings
Go right straight on for Jennings
You are now one mile from Jennings
That is Jennings, up the block

So that when we came to a little town it was rather an experience to see the real house of Jennings, with the door open, and no doubt the real Jennings inside, filling people's Thermos flasks, and all sorts of soul kisses floating about in the atmosphere from the happy pasts of lovers. But we only looked at Jennings. We went for our cold drink to some much humbler place, and then like the people in the story we passed by on the other side.

This is a strange old Spanish town, built by the Missions, and there are strange Moorish-looking buildings here, and a foreign-smell and colour and flavour, and a great deal of Spanish in the shops and in the streets, and notices in Spanish on the walls. I very nearly came to live here as a boy, many years ago, and was only kept from coming here, by a chance, so that it is interesting to me to be here and to see it now under such different conditions.

All greetings to you. I hope that you aren't having too rough a time. All pleasant blessings attend you.

Yours always sincerely   *John Masefield*

59   *21 March*   *Hotel Alexandria, Los Angeles*

Dear Margaret, I wrote to you last from San Antonio, which was a place with rather more flavour than this, though this is more famous, being a kind of Riviera, with mountains, and eternal snows, and orange groves, and the smell of lemon trees, and palms and flowers. The Pacific is only 10 miles away, and Drake sailed up this coast about 1580, in his voyage round the world, and wintered in a secret harbour here, and no other white men came for 2 centuries.

Last week-end, I was driven down into the Californian desert, which is a wonderful place, where one would like to live (like Shelley) 'forever'. It is strange how lonely places win the souls of people. Mountaineers and desert people are always passionately fond of their rocks and sands, and when one sees the desert and the desert mountains one understands why the poor Indians fought for them as they did.

The mountains are immense craggy bulks, with gigantic pines on them, and snows, and rocky cañons or gullies, filled with torrents, and Indian devils who cry out at night. In the torrent beds there are great palm trees, and then on the desert itself there are soft, grey-green, grey-brown, grey-blue trees and bushes and cactuses, nearly all thorny, sage brush, and smoke-trees, and mezquite, and a sort of mimosa, more beautiful than anything can say, in the desert light.

You look across the desert at the sandy mountains beyond, which seem only 5 miles away, but are really 30 miles, and you see nothing but sand, and scrub, and boulders, and you long to be there 'forever', and all the snakes and wildcats and other terrors, seem to fit into the scheme of life, and the tales of the devils in the cañons seem true, and you don't want to test them. And then you stand and listen and hear no solitary thing for hours and hours, and little silent ratty beasts called gophers come out and run on the sand.

On the way to the desert, you go through rocky defiles and passes, all painted with advertisements, thus:

Prepare to meet thy God

Gee, that's great candy. Its Hickses

Jesus is coming

Mind Your Liver. Does your Liver run right?

Jesus is coming

Painless Parker. Teeth without Tears.

Jesus is coming

Pete's Pills cured me. They'll cure you.

Jesus is coming

Prepare to meet thy God

All the show parts of Calif are lovely, the orange groves and the snowy mountains and the light, but nothing comes up to the desert, where the Indians still dance their dances, and their devils still live. I wish you could all have been there. What a time we would have had there. Women wear men's clothes there and cut their hair short, and at first you think there are no women there at all, so you often have to watch, to see if they spit, and then if they do they are men.

All good wishes to you my dear Margaret. I hope that you are having a happy time in your work.

Yours sincerely   *John Masefield*

60   *29 March*   *The Portland, Portland, Oregon*

Dear Margaret, It was a great pleasure to get your letter two days ago in San Francisco. So many thanks for it.

I couldn't write in San Francisco, as it is a feverish place, and I had to speak twice in 36 hours, and give not less than seven interviews. It is a strange place, on flattish ground near a vast harbour, and when I was there it was all overcast with a kind of a forbidding dismal grue, for it is all shut in with hills of a dismal kind, covered with fir trees; and cloud rolls down and covers the hills, and it seems then as though all hope were gone, and as though the sky would extinguish any grace or life or hope forever and ever. I think I was more weary in SF than in any place I have ever seen. It used to be a very wicked place when I was a boy at sea, for the crimps (or dealers in sailors) there used to take men by force, and drug them or beat them senseless, and then sell them to ships in need of crews. But all this is over now, and I went at night down one of the worst of all the old sailors' haunts and found it as tame as Wootton*; a few rifle saloons, and a quiet little dance hall, and 2 or 3 quiet men talking politics, all the old violence and drunkenness and murder completely gone. And only 25 years ago, it was dangerous for any man to enter the street by night, and not over safe by day.

After leaving San Francisco, I had a dismal journey north to this place, dismal because I was trainsick, which was a new experience, and very harrowing, for it is just like sea-s, only worse, because one does not expect it. The train was going like this ⌒⌒⌒ all day long, round the curves of mountains, and it was horrid, except at one place, where it stopped. Then we all got out, — O my dear Margaret there was a miraculous waterfall of pure magnesia tumbling over the hill all ready mixed, and as cold as lovely ice. And all poor train-sick sufferers rushed at this lovely fall and lapped the health-giving stream just like Israelites at the rock in a picture, and I drank about a quart, because anyway, even if it were poison, it would be different from being sick, and it was all cold and had a nice sort of minerally-greasy taste, and there were little bubbles in it, and it came gushing down from the crags with such a rush and beauty and freshness that I longed to bathe in it and never get into the trains again.

Then presently we came to this place where I have spoken 3 times so far, in 30 hours; and tonight I go out by the midnight, further to the north. In a week from now I shall be turning east again, and should be in Chicago in about 10 days, and in 16 days in New York. They may send me round on a second journey though, to all the camps.

My dear Margaret, I hope that you will find the eastern counties pleasant, and that you will keep well and have Edward with you from time to time. Perhaps you are at Boar's Hill now, for Easter.

All greetings to you wherever you may be.

Yours ever   *John Masefield*

61   *2 April*   *In Seattle*

My dear Margaret, I don't think that I could describe the beauty before me, as I write.

I am on the 8th floor of a big hotel, overlooking Puget Sound, and it is a faultless day, with sun, and a brisk breeze, and the Sound is full of ships, a full-rigged ship and a big schooner are just towing in, and a big steamer is just steaming out, and the Sound is a pale blue, and beyond it are low hills covered with pines, dark blue in the haze, and beyond those are a wall of mountains the colour of the Sound, and above those, in the faint-coloured sky, are amazing snowy peaks going on forever.

However, one takes little joy in all this beauty, while the battle rages* in France. People have been very panicky here; and though I feel pretty downcast, I don't let them see it, and I tell them, whenever I speak each night, to buck up, and to be confident, and so latterly I have felt that I have been of some little use.

I don't think I shall get home this Spring. I expect I shall have to go round all the Camps here first, which will mean another ten or fifteen thousand miles in the train, this time in the heat, instead of in the cold. If this happens, I will try to write to you more regularly, as you are a nice person and ought to have letters regularly, and you are a brick as well and write delightful letters back.

In my few odd moments, my mind shies away from the war to romance. I would love someday to write a nice romance, with beauty and adventure and tenderness and pathos and colour, and some kind of achievement through defeat in it. If this war should end some time, this would be a happy task for the first year of peace.

I hope you are having a pretty good time, in spite of the news and your change to the east. Keep well — if you ever have time, my dear, do please send me a line about yourself.

Yours ever   John Masefield

Did I tell you about the picnic in California? We went for a picnic up a Cañon, and presently, as we ate our picnic, the woodticks began upon us, and came creepy crawley up us, on their little neat flat bellies, like the serpent in Genesis. The tick is an adhesive beast, like the 1 in France, or like the remora, or sucker, which clings to ships; they are the devil at picnics. This is all about the tick at present.

We Danced

We danced away care till the fiddler's eyes blinked,
And at supper, at midnight, our wine-glasses chinked,
Then we danced till the roses that hung round the wall
Were broken red petals that did rise and did fall
To the ever-turning couples of the bright-eyed and gay,
Singing in the midnight to dance care away.

Then the dancing died out and the carriages came,
And the beauties took their cloaks and the men did the same.
And the wheels crunched the gravel and the lights were turned
    down,
And the tired beauties dozed through the cold drive to town.

Nan was the belle and she married her beau,
Who drank, and then beat her, and she died long ago,
And Mary, her sister, is married and gone
To a tea planter's lodge, in the plains, in Ceylon.

And Dorothy's sons have been killed out in France,
And Mary lost her man in the August advance,
And Em, the man jilted, and she lives all alone
In the house of this dance which seems burnt in my bone.

Margaret and Susan and Marion and Phyllis
With red lips laughing and the beauty of lilies
And the grace of wild swans and a wonder of bright hair,
Dancing among roses with petals in the air.

All, all are gone, and Hetty's little maid
Is so like her mother that it makes me afraid.
And Rosalind's son, whom I passed in the street,
Clinked on the pavement with the spurs on his feet.

62   *11 April*   *Hotel Marion, Marion, Ohio*

My dear Margaret, I arrived in this town at 6 this morning, in an April thaw, and all things sloshy. They had told me to expect a lovely little busy city; but it is the very moral of what one would imagine Gomorrah to have been; though the people chew tobacco more than they did in Gomorrah, and that rather takes the edge off them.

I am slowly working east again, and hope to be in New York on the 14th. There I shall learn, whether I am to go all round the States again, to speak in the camps, or come home.

The camps are wonderful cities, all laid out with electric light and hot and cold water. Each camp has a big theatre, a music hall, a moving picture theatre (or two), an hotel, a guest house, a rifle-range with moving targets, of the kind they used to have at fairs, and billiard rooms with fifty or sixty tables.

I am only sending you this note today, to say, that I am venturing to send you a few things, which I hope may reach you safely about the middle of May or so. You must share them with Edward, if they reach you. You must not mind my venturing to send them to you, for the chances are that they will never arrive. Still, if they do arrive, I hope they'll be pleasant to you.

Best greetings and good wishes to you. I hope that the pleasant April woods are being their best for you.

Yours ever   *John Masefield*

63   *12 April*   *In Rochester, NY*

My dear Margaret, You may care to have these unposted post-cards of Niagara; the two of the Rapids, one above, and the other (the more terrible), below, the Falls, are quite pretty. The whirl-pool Rapids below the Falls are the waters which Captain Webb* set out to swim. They are by much the most awful thing I have ever seen. The waves which you see are not waves, rolling along in the lollop of the current, as waves ought to roll. They are awful forces of water which suddenly boil up into the air after having been strangled underneath by going over the Falls two miles higher up; and the power with which they heave up and beat back to bite the other waves is sickening to see, and then the whole beastly boiling awful water goes along with a yell, and it seems to shout 'We're in hell, we're in hell, we're in hell, and we shall never get out.'

It gives one a turn, to think that a man really dared, of his own will, to dive into that water in a bathing-dress, and try to swim it.

He wasn't drowned. One big wave picked him up and crushed him dead against another wave.

I hope that the Censor won't bag these from you.

Yours ever   *John Masefield*

64   *17 April*   *Harvard Club, 27 West 44th Street, New York City*

My dear Margaret, So many thanks for your beautiful letter (March 22nd). It was a great pleasure to me to have it.

I am back in the East again, having gone all round the country, and am now waiting orders to go all round it a second time.

New York, in spite of the fever and excitement of the life here, is a very lovely city, and it was always, even in the days of hardship, when I was a boy*, a romantic and glamorous place, where almost anything might happen, and where the light and the life had a colour and a strangeness, very attractive to me. It would be attractive to you, I think, but the place I wish you could have been at was Oregon, for there the beauty was beyond all words, spring beginning on the forests and snowpeaks every-where, and the divine brooks singing in the divine air.

The men of Oregon are enormous, as their main task is handling giant pine trees. Sometimes they would smite me on the back after a speech, and I would have to go away and cough blood and have cold water sprinkled on me.

How I envy you seeing the English spring. I could hardly bear your description of the laughing of the snipe. They used to do it in the flat wet fields between Lollingdon and the station, where we so often walked, and I suppose they are doing it now; nearly the only laughter* in England now, my God.

I'm speaking about England here on the 23rd. It's St George's Day, and I want to do it well.

I hope to have news of you when the Easter letters come in. The mails take about 3 weeks each way now.

You were quite right about the hotel 'built for me to enjoy'. It was a whited sepulchre of a place really, tho it had its points after 18 hours in a filthy train.

You were very good and kind to write to me as you did. Thank you.

All greetings and good wishes to you. My service to Edward.
Yours ever   *John Masefield*

65   *15 May*   *Harvard Club*

My dear Margaret, Here is a little print of the ship Margaret, under easy plain sail, bound from Salem, Mass.

Will you please tell Edward, if you should see him that I have recently met a Capt. Wilsdon, of the O and BLI, who is now a flying officer of the Br Mission here, and engaged in some matter of aerial photography! I met him at Rochester, NY, about 360 miles from here, when I was speaking there last week. It was a great pleasure to me to hear about Edward so unexpectedly and in so far a corner. Capt. W desired to be remembered to him.

I sent you a pair of moccasins, in Indian beadwork, last week. I hope that they may reach you safely, and please you in some way, if not as footgear. It is a great trouble to me, that I never sent you any sweet things, as I might have before the order came. Now I cannot. Still, if I see any nice relic of this land I will try to send it to you.

The best greetings to Edward and you.
Always sincerely yours   *John Masefield*

66   *27 May*   *The Selwyn, Charlotte, NC*

Dear Margaret, I am doing one-night-stands at the different camps here, and am at present in what they call the South Eastern District, a place about as big as Europe with Russia left out. I am today at the above house, in one of the '75 with bath', feeling very superior to the mean trash who are in the 75 without.

It is about 100° hot today. A man of N Carolina was bragging about the heat of his State to a Texan the other day. He said, 'In N Carolina, it goes up to 120° in the shade.' 'Huh,' said the Texan. 'In Texas there ain't no shade.'

I don't feel the heat much yet, except in the trains at night, when I make long journeys by sleeper; then it is apt to be clammy.

By day I wear what is called a 'crash' suit. You must not think from the name that this is a loud suit. It is a sort of toga, made apparently of sacking; and as most of my hotels are strewn with cigar-ash, by the earlier occupants, you may say that I live in sackcloth and ashes.

This is the real South that fought the Civil War. Yesterday I was in the old Confederate capital, Richmond, where there was so much passion and heroic resolve in those old days. All this South Eastern District fought for four years, till every one was ruined, and most of the men dead, and most of the houses destroyed, and most of the fields out of cultivation. The land looks as tho' it had not recovered, even yet.

The camps are amazing places, with hotels for the soldiers' lady friends to stay at, and theatres, and movie-theatres, and rifle-ranges, where you can hit clay pigeons at a cent a go, and the most excellent huts and lecture halls, and generally a music hall as well, besides billiard rooms with 50 tables. They give the men a jolly good time here, and the men are splendid. It is a treat to talk to them.

The other night I spoke to a negro battalion. They were very nice and attentive and they seemed to like what I said, though I'd never spoken to negroes in bulk before. Afterwards they sang songs to me, and danced. The dances were just clog and step solo dances, clever, but not impressive. The songs moved me a great deal. I wished that you had been there to have heard them. I can't describe their wistful moaning melancholy. They seemed to say, 'O God, you've made us black men have brains of wool, O God, it's awful for us.' The songs were generally phrases repeated over and over with wistful, changing, moaning tunes. One of the best (a very lovely thing) was:

'Don't yo' hear them lil lambs bleating,/O Shepherd, feed my sheep?' and one, which drove the battalion crazy with joy, ran

> Little David he play on the harp,
>   Hallelu, Hallelu, Hallelu.
> Little Moses he stand an listen,
>   Hallelu, Hallelu, Hallelu.
> Little David he go on playing;
>   Hallelu, Hallelu, Hallelu.
> Little Holy Ghost he stand right dere.
>   Hallelu, Hallelu, Hallelu.

All good wishes to you. I hope you're in some nice leafy pleasant woodland, where the nightingales sing Hallelu.

Yours sincerely   *John Masefield*

67   *1 June*   *The Albion, Augusta, Ga*

My dear Margaret, Thank you so much for your nice letter of May 4th. It reached me yesterday in the hot, smelly, fly-ey, but very attractive city, of Charleston. It was a great pleasure to me to hear from you.

I wanted to send an answer yesterday, but could not quite manage it, as I had a busy day. I went out into a camp in a pine wood, and stood on a waggon, in the middle of a regiment in hollow square, who, like the shepherds watching their flocks, were all seated on the ground, in their formation. I spoke to them a good long time, and they were a jolly good audience, perhaps because their colonel was present. Then I went to the Navy Yard and talked (that is, spoke) to the sailors, and afterwards answered questions for an hour. They were splendid men. All this army and navy are superb. They are all as fine as the RND and the 1st Australian Division; splendid, alert, full of what is here called 'pep', and also full of initiative and invention. It is wonderful to think that this fresh and magnificent army is really entering France on our side.

While I was standing on the waggon, the beastly little mosquitoes got home on my ankles.

As to the Boche drive*; it was painful to be here, as a sort of official mouthpiece, while it was going on, and no news was coming through to help me to answer. I thought it all out, and came to a conclusion about it, and time has shewn that I was right on all points, and after that I was ready for all questioners, but it was a horrid shock, to find the Somme field gone, and Alberta the leaning Virgin gone, and Amiens being shelled to pieces, and I expect by this time poor little Mesmil church, that I bragged about, gone the way of Pozières and Beaumont Hamel.

This isn't a letter, but I want you to have my thanks for writing.

Bless you.

Yours ever   *John Masefield*

My dear Margaret, In your days in France, you may have heard an old Civil War Song about 'When we were marching through Georgia,' with the words: 'That is how we shouted from Atlanta to the sea.' Well, this is Atlanta, in the heart of Georgia, and if I were to sing the song in anything like a breezy style here I would get a bat on the head. Dixie is the only song in these parts.

I'm not sure, but I rather think that Georgia is short for George-the-Thirdia.

I've just come back from a hot and dusty camp, where I spoke for an hour in the open, with a thunderstorm for a background, and a great array of sitting soldiers below me. It is hard work to speak in the open in the dust. Tomorrow I shall have to do it twice or three times; but today was a slack day, which I passed mainly in writing and going to the movies. I went to 4 movies.

One of them was a movie of Gerard,* lately Ambassador to the Kaiser from this country. It shewed in pictures all that Gerard (if you have read his book) tells in words, and like the book, it makes jolly good propaganda, and throws rather a side light on little Kronprinz. It made little Kronprinz rather a sportsman, and much more attractive than Wilhelm.

Presently Gerard in the movey says: 'Rather than sign such a treaty, I would stay here till hell freezes.' This was a beau geste, and brought down the house.

Presently I went to another movey, which was against being wicked and drunken, and made a deep impression on me; and then I went to another which was all about a wicked Boche, (who hadn't gone to the above) who abducts a poor American lady in his submarine, and then I went to another, which was billed as 'Prunella or Love in a Dutch Garden* by Granville Ba[r]ker'.

It is probable that I told you about the movey city of Los Angeles. There all the movey-makers live, because within 50 miles of the city they can have every kind of country they can want, quite devilish desert, snowy mountains, torrents, rivers, fertile valleys, scrub, semitropical forest, the sea and ships, flat land, farm land and townland. So there you will see cities of all kinds, Babylonian, Chinese, Roman and Louis Quatorze, all with no backs to them, and there I saw the great Charlie Chaplin with his little Dogg Mutt. He was doing a play with Mutt*. The theory or fable of the play was, that he and Mutt should go to a rather tough music hall, and ask to be admitted, and be refused with contumely, on the principle, that no dogs are allowed. So he goes away, but is not discouraged, he has a brainstorm, puts the dog in his trousers and is admitted without a word. I am not sure whether this is wit or humour, but it is one of the two.

Now all good blessings attend you, in whatever green wood you walk.

Yours ever   *John Masefield*

I daresay the Censor will bag it, but if he doesn't, you may like to see the enclosed card, shewing Stone Mountain near here. It is rather a notable rocky skull, sticking out of the ground. I see it on my way out each day.

69   *12 June*   *The Battle House, Mobile, Ala*

Dear Margaret, A letter reached me a few days ago, which raised a hope in me, that I may be able to start home in a week or ten days from now. Probably this will not be. I expect I shall have another 8 weeks here.

This city is on one of the inlets of the gulf, and is on a flat stretch of wooded ground bordered by great creeks and rivers. It was a French city at one time, and Creole French is still spoken here, and at one time it was a main place for pirates, just as New Orleans was. When ships were small, these creeks made very good snug harbours. They could lay their ships on their sides here, to scrub them, and they could get very good new spars from the pine woods, and be safe from any kind of cruiser.

I go from camp to camp, still, talking to the men. Some of the notices in the huts are very fine; thus:

If you spit on the floor
At Home
Spit on the floor here
We want you to feel at home.

This under a picture of a gentleman who is making himself liberally at home in this particular way.

Then there is another, equally cutting, which runs:

Don't Expectorate on this floor
If you Expect to Rate as a Gentleman

When I have any time, which isn't often, I go to the movey

shows, and learn how to abduct an heiress in a submarine, or to rob a stage coach (in several different ways, this) and how to steal priceless despatches, and how to murder, with a knife, a pistol, poison or strangulation, and how to get somebody else into prison for it, which is even more important.

I think that movies are excellent for comedy and for the wilder kinds of excitement, where speed is a help but so far I don't feel that they offer anything else.

It is lovely to be in Alabama after being in Georgia. It is as lovely as its name. It is a vast expanse, much of it wild and awful, but much of it exquisite pasture, growing a kind of clover, called melilotis, 3 feet high, lovely to look at, lovely to smell, going on for miles and miles, green and grey and fragrant, and covered with a fluttering cloud of little yellow butterflies. You would love to be in the melilotis, hearing the negroes sing 'Swing low, sweet chariot,' and looking at the pines with your by this time professional eye.

Blessings and greetings to you. Yours always sincerely   *John Masefield*

70   *24 June*   *The Grunewald, New Orleans*

My dear Margaret, So many thanks for your two nice Devonshire letters, one from Widdicombe and one from near Princeton. They were like glimpses of England. One reached me in the wilds of Mississippi, in a temperature of 96°. The other reached me in New York in a temperature of 45°, only four days later. Now, after another four days, I am in 96° again.

It is most kind and good of you to write me such nice long letters full of lovely things about England. It is a very great pleasure to me to have them. Thank you very much indeed for them all.

I hope Tam Pearce's grey mare is not now a nightmare; and I hope Danl Whiddon and Uncle Tom Cobbleigh keep pretty well.

I never was on Dartmoor, but I've seen it, from the north, going to Cornwall, and from the south, when I used to go to stay near the Lea at Slapton. It used to make a northern horizon there, and one could see it, austere and big, over the fat lands and woods nearer the sea. The last time I saw it was on a transport going along the coast. One saw it as a kind of rim to the south coast, almost the last thing we saw as we left the land.

I've copied out for you some verses about the female friend. I hope they'll amuse you. They are by a gallant man called Cornelius Ussher, who was probably a curate in our Church, by the sound of him.

Down in Alabama last week (Alabama is said to mean Here we rest) I saw an elderly negress in the process of being saved. She had been to a revival and had come home giggling and much excited, greatly to the disgust of her mistress, who knew from experience, that a maid who is being saved does not work while it lasts. The woman kept saying; 'O, Miss Anne, I bein' washed in de Blood. I gwine ter be saved. De dear Lawd he forgive ole Marfa. I goin ter get salvation.'

'Dat's right, Marfa,' said her friends, 'Go on, Marfa. Keep on, Marfa. Go on right up to de trone. Press on to de Lawd, Marfa. You bin a drefful sinner, Marfa, now you be wash in de Blood you be jes' like one lil lamb.'

They reminded me very much of some boys whom I once saw encouraging two dogs to fight.

Here are some verses about travelling in a sleeper in these hot parts:

> The night is burning and long
> The engine drones his song
> The brakes complain
> To the coupling chain
> And the wheels say both are wrong
> I lie again in my bunk
> The train shakes as though drunk
> Not a breath of air
> Comes to me there
> But the wheels below go Clunk
> A man comes brushing past
> And the porter follows fast.
> In the bunk next mine
> Is a snoring pig
> I wish this breath were his last
> In the bunk beyond is a child
> Which has not yet been beguiled
> Into being wise

And shutting its eyes
Obeying its mother mild.
It is driving its mother wild.
And beyond, there comes a wail
'Adèle, Adèle, Adèle,
Did you take those pills
Of Doctor Wills
To make pink people pale?'
And Adèle replies from afar
'O, you woke me up, Mamma.
I packed the pills
With my Sunday frills
In the trunk in the baggage car.'
So when Adèle has been strafed,
And the neighbours have cursed or laughed,
I try again
To compose my brain
To prevent my going daft
The train goes on in the night
The moon outside is white
Its a hundred and six
Which is hotter than Styx
And the she-mosquitoes bite.
They suck till they're full of blood,
Then they linger, chewing the cud
Then their greedy brain
Makes them bite again
And none of their bites is a dud.
And the train goes moaning and griding
And in the wood at a siding
I see in the dark
The fireflies spark
And a great deer go to hiding.

All greetings to you. Bless you. Always yours very sincerely,
John Masefield

In this imperfect, gloomy scene
Of complicated ill,
How rarely is a day serene,
The throbbing bosom still!

Will not a beauteous landscape bright,
Or music's soothing sound,
Console the heart, afford delight,
And throw sweet peace around?

They may, but never comfort lend
Like an accomplished female friend.

With such a friend the social hour
In sweetest pleasure glides:
There is in female charms a power
Which lastingly abides
The fragrance of the blushing rose,
Its tints and splendid hue,
Will with the season decompose
And pass as early dew.

On firmer ties his joys depend
Who has a polished female friend.

As orbs revolve and years recede,
And seasons onward roll,
The fancies may on beauties feed
With discontented soul.
A thousand objects bright and fair
May for a moment shine
Yet many a sigh and many a tear
But mark their swift decline.

While lasting joys the man attend
Who has a faithful female friend.

71   *26 June*   *Hotel Bentley, Alexandria, La.*

My dear Margaret, The Niagara p pcards reached you safely, so I
am sending you just these few, shewing scenes in this cotton
country in the South. They are rather good cards, and they may
amuse you and shew you the kind of thing the south is. The
cotton is only green so far. I shall not see it in its white and fluffy

stage. I suppose it looks, really, rather like the Irish bog cotton, only much taller and handsomer. In its present stage it looks like heliotrope, or very young runner bean, or young potato plant, about 1 foot high.

I was in New Orleans yesterday, but was speaking all day long and saw very little of the city. It is a vast city, and does a trade with central and South America, and a great deal of French and Spanish is spoken in the streets; and one sees nice old familiar signs in the roads near the docks.

'John Rawlings
Sailmaker and Rigger
Handmade and Machine Made sails'

'Old Joe
The Reliable Sailmaker'

'Young Peter Henderson
The Sailmaker with Pep'

'Do you want them fine Sails?
Go to Dick's
George. W. Dick
The Rigger with the Punch.'

Very soon, I shall call on Young Mr Henderson and Geo. W. Dick, and ask them for sails to take me home. For I may be sailing this day five weeks. It is too wonderful to think of.

All greetings to you, from this far and hot and lonely place, on its red and muddy river. I hope the cards may reach you safely.

Your letters have been a great pleasure to me. Thank you so much for writing. Yours ever   *John Masefield*

I still go to the movies now and then. I've learned how to murder, with knife, poison, revolver, and strangulation: how to abduct, with chloroform, a submarine, or a good wooden bat on the head: how to rob a stage coach, full face and profile, how to blow up a munitions factory, break a man's back, garotte in a back alley, fling a man out of a window, burgle a house, kidnap an inventor, and drug a dinner party.

'In a heart less pure than mine such seed would raise a strange crop.'

Elizabeth Daryush

Armistice

On this day of longed-for peace
With the joy-peals bursting free,
What shall give our thoughts release?

Surge they with the city's glee
Press they like the charging crowd
Clamorous or strangely proud.

Wild-eyed women, mourners sad,
War-worn fighters, maimed & bowed,
Drunkards riotously mad,

Youths & girls who jest & sing,
Children frolicsome & loud,
Staring too & wondering,

Or above the town, on high
Airships, reconnoitreing,
All day, in the silent sky.

Elizabeth Daryush

72 *20 January*

Dear Margaret, I have been trying to get light on what is troubling you.

The judgment of the world is roughly right on many points. It is (roughly) against marriage* between persons of greatly differing ages. The experience and feeling of the world is against such a marriage. Special persons make special cases of such marriage very happy and successful. You are a special person, and it might be so in your case; but marriage is a difficult art, even when there is no disparity, and the disparity adds to the difficulty in many ways.

Firstly and mainly, perhaps, in the way of which I tried to speak last night, that the elder person knows so much more about the game of life. Twenty years is a great space of time between 30 and 50. In it, one passes from the adventurous and experimental stage, in which you are now, (that is, the beauty-making stage, when, in the main, each generation adds what it has to add to the glory of the world) into the riper age, of greater mental power but less fire, in which people crystallize, and thence into the steady stage, of judgment, tranquil enjoyment, and unwillingness to move, which precedes decline.

In a marriage in which there is this disparity, the older has this advantage, or disadvantage, that he or she has already gone over the ground that the younger is travelling, and may therefore be impatient, and may rate as defects what are simply the results of being in an earlier, perhaps a lovelier, stage. The younger has not only to become accustomed to the loss of independence, which all men and women feel a little, however deeply they may love, but to the loss of his or her standards, of friends and life and thought and art. In these things experience has a way of over-riding instinct, and even if this be beneficial in particular instances, it is too sudden and too wrenching to seem so, at first.

I suppose that the perfect marriage would be a shared and equal delight in the equal discovery of life. In the marriage of young and old, the older can say, 'You need not go down that road. I have been down it, and have returned.'

Then, the great happiness of marriage, apart from the happiness of having an anchorage, and companionship, and the aim which these things give, is the happiness of having children. In marrying, one must think of the possible children. A disadvantage, in a marriage between old and young, is, that the older parent may be too old (in mind and disposition) to be a help to the children when they want him most, in youth, which is always so difficult. Emotional response becomes weaker as one grows older, 'one cannot be bothered', so that the children miss something, even if the other parent does not.

One of the reasons which have made me curse the war has been this, that it has perhaps kept you from meeting and marrying the very perfect man I have longed for you to have. You are so beautiful and wonderful that I have deeply longed to see you make the very happiest, most perfect and most lovely marriage that can be. If this, now in your thought, is to be your choice, I hope that it may be that.

Trust your instinct more than your thought. I am sure that a beautiful life will come to you. This may be that life. Perhaps it only seems so at the minute, as something steady and sure in the midst of all this driving, which has torn you up by the roots.

Don't think that you must take this, because a refusal will cause pain. It may cause pain, but a generous pain, that men are often the nobler for. It is a decision of your whole nature, an act of you. That can only be reverenced and respected. It is a decision of a soul.

Then your thought, 'that it might be well, even if it were unhappy.' That did not make me happy to hear. That did not seem the word I would like to be saying before your marriage.

Well, dear, I'm not adding to what I said. Forgive this, if it is all blundering and amiss. You are all beautiful and glorious, so that I can't think of unhappiness ever touching you. I can only think of very beautiful things coming to you and making you very happy in all ways and in all things. So may these things come to you.

May whatever there is of wisdom and beauty to help us in our trouble be with you now. Yours ever, *John Masefield*

73   *25 January*

Dear Margaret, Thank you for your letter. We are very good friends, you and I.

I see all your side of it, I think. Perhaps when I talked with you and wrote to you I did not get enough of you into the picture.

Some of the happiest marriages I have seen have been marriages of disparity, of age; in one case 25 years difference. They have succeeded, perhaps, because with the unusual case you have the unusual person, and with the unusual person you have imagination, which is, in the main, having the mind and the will to wise ways in things.

No amount of parity will make marriage, or life itself, easy. It is as hard a thing as art. It is living at close range, being unselfish with one toothbrush and musical with the bailiffs in. And, like a work of art, it isn't, in the main, just delight, but, in the main, hard thought and the will to perfection, the senses of power and of style, in which the artist, even the greatest, has to say, 'als ich Kanne'.

I am sure that you would make a right and good and beautiful thing, of this marriage. The woman sets the tone of a home. The woman is the artist, the home and the man are her clay and her colours. You would make a very beautiful home and man. I am very sure of that.

Many years ago, I was very much struck by some lines of Browning*:

> The common problem —
> Is, not to fancy what were fair in life,
> Provided it could be, but to find out
> What can be, first, and then to make that fair.
> A very different thing . . .

It has always seemed to me to be very wise. We do not live in any land of Trapalanda, but right here and now, with men and women of flesh and blood and all manner of roughness and loveliness, working on each other to some end of justice and medicine for each of us, wise and good in the main, though strange enough.

You would get much, and live deeply and beautifully, and bring quiet and beauty and happiness in any man's home.

I've always thought, that the thoughts of men and women

make angels, which go about those whom people love, to help and calm and guard them. So may all manner of beautiful thoughts be about you, from all good people, in these days, and help you into your life's way. Yours   *John Masefield*

We saw your Father and Mother today, both very well, and 'moved in' and living in the schoolroom.

Notes

Introduction See Constance Babington Smith, *John Masefield: A Life* (Oxford University Press, 1978), p. 183, a volume to which this editor is deeply indebted.

Letters (JM = John Masefield; MB = Margaret Bridges)

3 *Cholsey* In the summer of 1914 the Masefields (JM, his wife Constance, and their two children) moved into Lollingford Farm, Cholsey, about two miles south of Wallingford, in the Thames Valley, at the edge of the Berkshire Downs. *Argonne thing* In the spring of 1915 JM formed a plan to establish a travelling field hospital behind the Army of the Argonne, and in July he spent two weeks touring military hospitals in the Tours area, to guide him in setting up fresh-air hospitals. Nothing came of this project. Instead JM went to Gallipoli for the Red Cross in the late summer of 1915; and in early 1916 he visited the United States on a lecture tour — see Introduction.

5 *Well Walk* The Masefields took the house at 13 Well Walk, Hampstead, in 1912, and maintained it as their town residence until 1917. *Hill Crest* The Masefields moved into Hill Crest, Boar's Hill, Oxford, in April 1917. *Judith* (1904–) JM's first child and only daughter. *Mr Waterhouse* Probably Paul Waterhouse (1861–1925), son of the architect Alfred Waterhouse (1830–1905) whose daughter Monica (1863–1949) was the wife of Robert Bridges. *Bridges household* Robert Bridges (1844–1930); his family moved into their house, Chilswell, Boar's Hill, Oxford, in 1907. *Con* JM's wife Constance, *née* de la Cherois Crommelin (1867–1960). *Lewis* (1910–42) JM's only son. *Mr Britling sees it through* by H.G. Wells (1866–1946) (Cassell; Macmillan, New York, 1916). *Good Friday: a play in verse* (Letchworth, Garden City Press, 1916). The play was produced at the Garrick Theatre, London, on 25 February 1917.

6 *This place* JM has just begun his fourth trip to France during the war period. He is in the Somme area for the purpose of writing his chronicles of the Battle of the Somme (1 July–18 November 1916) in which the British lost over 400,000 men. On an earlier trip to the Somme in October 1916, when the battle was still raging, Masefield had been commissioned by General (later Field Marshal) Sir Douglas Haig to write an account of the conflict. Two books resulted from these expeditions: *The Old Front Line, or the beginning of the Battle of the Somme* (Heinemann; Macmillan, New York, 1917) and *The Battle of the Somme* (Heinemann, 1919). *Arc-en-Barrois* In February and March 1915 JM spent six weeks as an orderly at the British Red Cross hospital for French wounded, which was in the château at Arc-en-Barrois, near Chaumont.

7 *Edward* Brother of MB. Captain Edward Ettingdene Bridges (1892–1969), of the Oxfordshire and Buckinghamshire Light Infantry, who was at the front at this time. He was wounded in France in February 1917. He later became the first Lord Bridges.

8 *Albert* An important road centre in the Somme area, on the main road and direct railway-line to Amiens. *Thiepval* A village in the Somme area devastated by the Battle of the Somme. *Elizabeth* Elizabeth Daryush, *née* Bridges (1887–1977), elder sister of MB.

11 *Blighty* British slang for 'home' or 'homeland', derived from the Hindi 'bilayati' meaning 'English'. It originated as service slang among British soldiers in India. It was also used as a term for a wound which would require a soldier's return to England. A comic trench journal published by British soldiers was called *Blighty*. Noel Coward wrote the song, 'Take me back to dear old Blighty'. *Bapaume* A town of strategic importance in the Somme area, goal of much of the fighting.

14 *old battalion* Edward Bridges served with the 1st/14th battalion (Territorial) of the Ox. and Bucks. Light Infantry. *Anzacs* Soldiers of the Australian and New Zealand Expeditionary Force. *Brooke's battalion* On 27 September 1914 Rupert Brooke was commissioned as sub-lieutenant in command of the 15th Platoon, D Company, Anson Battalion, Second Naval

Brigade — a land force. In November 1914 he was cross-posted to Hood Battalion, as sub-lieutenant in charge of No. 3 Platoon, A company, commanded by Lieutenant Freyberg. JM's reference is to the Hood Battalion which by the end of June 1915 had lost at Gallipoli eleven of its fifteen officers. *daredevil Freyberg*   Bernard Cyril Freyberg, 1st Baron (1889–1963), born in London but taken as a child to New Zealand. During the landings by British forces on the Gallipoli peninsula on 25 April 1915, Lieutenant Freyberg swam ashore at Bulair from a destroyer, towing a raft of flares which he posted at intervals along the coast. Thinking an attack was in progress, the Turks kept an army at Bulair which should have been deployed elsewhere (see Masefield, *Gallipoli*, pp. 44–45 — Heinemann; Macmillan, New York, 1916). Freyberg went on to distinguish himself in France, where he won the Victoria Cross. In World War II he commanded the New Zealand Expeditionary Force. He was Governor-General of New Zealand 1946–52.

16   *The Russian coup*   On 10 March 1917 there was a general mutiny of the Russian troops at Petrograd. On 12 March a provisional government was formed. On 15 March Czar Nicholas abdicated in favour of his brother Michael, who in turn abdicated on 16 March.

17   *de Vigny*   Alfred Victor de Vigny (1797–1863), French poet, playwright, novelist, one of the leaders of the Romantic movement. *Anatole France* pseudonym of Jacques Anatole Thibault (1844–1924). *Histoire Comique* Anatole France's *Histoire Comique* (1903), translated as *A Mummer's Tale* (Dodd, Mead, New York, 1908) tells the story of a beautiful actress at the Odéon and the Théâtre Français who is threatened by the spirit of her former lover (a suicide) each time she is ready to give herself to her new lover, a diplomat. *Poincaré* Raymond Poincaré (1960–1934), President of the Third Republic 1913–20. *America is 'in'* Written as a postscript at the top of page one of this letter. America officially declared war on Germany on 6 April 1917, but the United States Senate had passed the resolution on 4 April. JM had probably heard of the Senate resolution just before posting the letter.

18   *An Anatole*   Probably Anatole France's *Les Dieux ont soif*

(1912), authorized translation by Alfred Allinson, *The Gods Are Athirst* (John Lane, 1913), a novel of the French Revolution which shows how the best causes can be spoiled by fanaticism.

19 *Arras* The first Battle of Arras took place 9 April–4 May 1917. After a bombardment and gas attack the British advanced four miles. The Canadians took Vimy Ridge. *Ypres* In the second Battle of Ypres (22 April–25 May 1915) chlorine gas was used for the first time by Germans.

20 *Hébuterne* A large village close to the front lines during the Battle of the Somme. It was shelled continuously for two years. *July 1st* The Battle of the Somme began on 1 July 1916.

22 *an Anatole* Probably *Le Procurateur de Judée* (1902), translated by Jessup, *The Procurator of Judea* (Macmillan, New York, 1929).

26 *Karalenko* Vladimir Korolenko (1853–1921), as the name is usually spelt, was a Russian populist writer, genial and humane in spite of his long exile in Siberia and northern Russia. Many of his stories are set in Siberia.

27 *the Revolution story* Anatole France's *Les Dieux ont soif* — see letter 18.

29 *Gatti's* This large Italo-Swiss café-restaurant was the only caterer serving the suburbs at the turn of the century. It was popular in the 1910s and 1920s.

31 *green wood. . .'Maid Margaret'* The greenwood is usually considered the territory of Robin Hood, but of course the phrase occurs elsewhere in ballads, as does the name Margaret or 'May Margaret'.

32 *war was declared* Austria declared war on Serbia on 28 July 1914. England declared war on Germany on 4 August 1914.

33 *Bagley Wood* It is about two miles south-east of the Masefield and Bridges homes on Boar's Hill. In his poem 'The Scholar-Gipsy' Matthew Arnold mentions it as the haunt of gypsies.

34 *the Asquiths*   Herbert Henry Asquith, first Earl of Oxford and Asquith (1852–1928), Prime Minister 1908–1916; his wife Margot, *née* Tennant, and his daughter Violet, Lady Bonham-Carter.

35 *Radnorshire*   A county in central Wales noted for its Radnor Forest. *Arthur Ransome* (1884–1967) was author of *Six Weeks in Russia in 1919* (Allen & Unwin, 1919), and later of children's books.

36 *the cottage*   The Bridges' house, Chilswell, suffered severe damage by fire on 6 February 1917. At the time of this letter Bridges and his wife were living in a cottage close by Chilswell. *Walpole*   Hugh Walpole (1884–1941), novelist.   *Nevinson* Henry Woodd Nevinson (1856–1941), essayist, philanthropist, journalist; author of books on Herder, Goethe, and Schiller. He had a scientific interest in military history and he was a war correspondent for thirty years at most of the wars of his time, including the Dardanelles campaign where he was wounded. His *The Dardanelles Campaign* (Nisbet, 1918) is a standard book. His friendship with JM resulted in *John Masefield: an appreciation, together with a bibliography* (Heinemann, 1931). *Crickhowell* (Howell's rock), Breconshire, south-central Wales, a picturesque village on a hill between Brecon and Abergavenny.

37 *the Galsworthys*   John Galsworthy (1867–1933), novelist, author of *The Forsyte Saga* (1906–21), and his wife. *Shaw's windows* George Bernard Shaw (1856–1950), playwright.

38 *Black Mountains*   The Black Mountains in Breconshire, Wales, which rise above the lovely Rhingall valley, are famous for their scenic beauty. *HW*   Hugh Walpole. *about Russia*   This letter was written during the Kornilov attack (9–14 September 1917) upon Kerensky's provisional government. Kornilov was defeated but at the cost of increased Bolshevik influence. A few weeks later (6 November) the Bolsheviks came to power with the storming of the Winter Palace in Petrograd. On 7 November the Bolsheviks published a Decree of Peace. On 5 December an armistice was concluded between Russia and the Central Powers, and on 3 March 1918 the Treaty of Brest-Litovsk was signed, which took Russia out of World War I. *The Brothers Karamazov* (1880), by Feodor Dostoevsky (1821–81).

39 *Smuts* Field Marshal the Rt Hon. Jan Christian Smuts (1870–1950), South African statesman. In World War I he commanded the Imperial Forces in South Africa, and was South Africa's representative in the Imperial War Cabinet in 1917 and 1918. Robert Bridges first met him in the later summer of 1917 when Smuts invited him and his son Edward, who was recovering from a war wound, to his rooms at the Savoy Hotel, London. They became friends and Smuts visited Chilswell several times. Bridges dedicated *October, and other poems* (1920) to him. *a play The Foundations,* which opened at the Gaiety Theatre on 8 October 1917. It received a favourable review in the *Manchester Guardian,* 9 October 1917. *to America again* JM's second visit to America to lecture on the war effort took place January–August 1918. *sack of Washington* During the War of 1812 the British set fire to the White House, the Capitol, and other buildings, 24–25 August 1814. *the Alabama* One of several British-built Confederate raiders which harassed Union shipping during the Civil War. In August 1872 the United States was awarded payment by Great Britain of $15,500,000 for damages resulting from the war action of the *Alabama* and other raiders.

40 *Granville-Barker* Harley Granville-Barker (1877–1946) was an actor, dramatist, and theatrical producer. He produced one of JM's earliest plays, 'The Tragedy of Nan', at the Court Theatre in 1908. Thereafter he exerted considerable influence on JM's career as a playwright. *Salisbury Antiphonal . . . Spirit of Man The Spirit of Man* (Longmans Green, 1916) was a wartime anthology compiled by Robert Bridges. Item 417, which begins 'Arm yourselves, and be ye men of valour', is taken from the *Salisbury Antiphoner* as translated by G. H. Palmer. *ruins of the house* Because of the fire of 1917 — see letter 36n. *South Wind* by Norman Douglas (1868–1952) (Secker, 1917). *The Loom of Youth* by Alec Waugh (Grant Richards, 1917).

41 *first American division* The first American troops to go to the front were units of the 1st Division which moved into the Toul sector on 21 October 1917. *Lady R* Probably Lady Rothschild or Lady Raleigh. *Tolstoi diaries* The *Manchester Guardian,* 1 October 1917, reviewed *The Diaries of Leo Tolstoy,* vol. 1, *Youth, 1847–52,* translated by C. J. Hogarth and A. Sirnis (Dent, 1917). *Tolstoi property* 'Bands of peasants have pillaged a portion of the

Yasnaya Polyana estate. The Countess Tolstoy has requested the Minister of the Interior to protect the property against any further devastation.' *The Times*, 8 October 1917. *The Soul of a Bishop* A novel by H. G. Wells (Cassell, 1917). *the Raleighs* Probably Sir Walter Alexander Raleigh (1862–1922) and his wife. He was Professor of English Literature at Oxford from 1904 on. *The Kaleidoscope* A novel by the Hon. Mrs Mary Frances Dowdall (1876–1939) (Duckworth, 1915). *Sorley's poems Marlborough, and other poems* by Charles Hamilton Sorley (1895–1915) (Cambridge University Press, 1916). *Vernede's War Poems, and Other Verses* by Robert Ernest Vernede (1875–1917) (Heinemann, 1917). *posthumous Swinburne The Posthumous Poems* by Algernon Charles Swinburne (1837–1909), edited by Edmund Gosse and T. J. Wise (Heinemann, 1917). *Beyond* A novel by John Galsworthy (Heinemann, 1917).

42 *Talgarth* Small town at the foot of the Black Mountains, Breconshire. *re-pointing* On 29 January 1918 the New College Choir, Oxford, gave a successful performance of the Psalms sung to Robert Bridges' new system of pointing.

43 *William* William II (1859–1941), the German Emperor. *Gosse* Sir Edmund Gosse (1849–1928), critic, literary historian and poet. *Asquith* — see letter 34n. *Harley* Harley Granville-Barker — see letter 40n.

44 *Salt and Savour* A novel by Mrs (Alfred) Cecil (Ullman) Sidgwick (?–1934) (Methuen, 1916). *Tino* Constantine I (1868–1923), King of the Hellenes and sovereign of the modern kingdom of Greece, on the throne 1913–17 and 1920–22. In 1889 he married Sophia (1870–1932), sister of the German Emperor William II and grand-daughter of Queen Victoria. *God and I God the Invisible King*, a novel by H. G. Wells (Cassell, 1917). *The Research Magnificent* (Macmillan, 1915). *The Passionate Friends* (Macmillan, 1913). *The Oilskin Packet: a tale of the southern seas*, a novel by Reginald Cheyne Berkeley and James Dixon (Duckworth, 1917).

45 *Bessie* Nurse to the Masefield family. *gloom about Italy* During the Caporetto campaign (24 October–26 December 1917) the Italians retreated to Piave under attack from German-Austrian forces, losing about 300,000 men taken prisoner and

more than that in deserters. *Lloydie*   David Lloyd George, first
Earl Lloyd-George of Dwyfor (1863–1945) Prime Minister 1916–
22. *Sinclair's book King Coal*, a novel by Upton Sinclair (1878–1968)
(Hutchinson; Macmillan, New York, 1917). *Chicago book* Upton
Sinclair, *The Jungle* (Heinemann; Doubleday, Page, 1906). *3 plays*
Granny Maumee, The Rider of Dreams, Simon the Cyrenian: plays for a
negro theater, by Frederick Ridgley Torrence (1875–1950)
(Macmillan, New York, 1917). *Mackenzie*   Compton Mackenzie
(1883–1972), novelist. JM probably had in mind his two-volume
novel, *Sinister Street* (Martin Secker, 1913–14) — see letter 45.
Keats in Scotland   In a letter addressed to Fanny Keats from
Dumfries, 2 July 1818, discussing his fatigue after a day of his
walking tour of the Lakes and the Highlands with his friend Mr
Brown, John Keats wrote: 'Then I get so hungry a Ham goes but a
very little way and fowls are like Larks to me. . .'. See H. Buxton
Forman, ed., *The Poetical Works and Other Writings of John Keats*, 4
vols., (Reeves & Turner, 1884) 3, p. 168.

46   *Brecon*   Town in Breconshire, south Wales, near the con-
fluence of the Tarrell and the Honddu rivers with the Usk.
Usk   The river Usk is considered one of the most beautiful rivers
in the United Kingdom; it flows from Carmarthen Van to the
Bristol Channel. *Towy*   The valley of the Towy, thirty miles long,
crosses Carmarthenshire. The beautiful woods and grassy hills
are famous in Welsh history and song.

48   *a couplet*   'Gheluvelt, Epitaph on the Worcesters, 31 October
1914', 'Askest thou of these graves? They'll tell thee, O stranger,
in England/How we Worcesters lie where we redeem'd the
battle.' In the Bridges Papers in the Bodleian Library, Oxford,
there is the following note by Edward Bridges on this poem:
'During the first battle of Ypres, the Germans on 31 October 1914,
attacked in overwhelming force the British line round Gheluvelt,
and captured a considerable section of our front line. The position
was critical. The 2nd Worcesters, from a support position,
counterattacked without, I believe, waiting for orders from the
higher command, and recaptured most of the front line which
had been lost. The attack was carried out with the greatest gal-
lantry, but with very heavy casualties. Robert Bridges' lines are,
of course, a conversion of Simonides' famous epitaph' [Go, tell
the Spartans, thou who passest by,/That here obedient to their

laws we lie.]. *Victory: an island tale* by Joseph Conrad (1857–1924) (Methuen; Doubleday, Page, 1915).

49 *Italian business* The retreat from Caporetto — see letter 45. *late PM* Herbert Asquith, who was replaced as Prime Minister by Lloyd George in 1916. *Kerensky* Alexander Kerenski (1881–1970), Russian socialist leader who became premier of the provisional government in July 1917. He was driven from power by the Bolsheviks on 6 November 1917, at the storming of the Winter Palace, St Petersburg. *Mackenzie books* *Guy and Pauline* (Martin Secker, 1915); *Carnival* (Martin Secker, 1912) — see letter 45. *a little theatre* This project was fully realized. Immediately after the war JM organized amateur theatricals in which his daughter Judith played an important part. Productions began in 1919 in the village of Wootton, near Oxford. The Hill Players was formed in 1922. The Music Room, a small theatre, was built close to Hill Crest in 1924. Experimental plays by W. B. Yeats, T. Sturge Moore, Laurence Binyon, JM and others, were performed here until 1932.

50 *Aberystwith* A popular Welsh resort on Cardigan Bay. *Llandrindod Wells* A well-known spa, first discovered in the reign of King Charles II, in the Upper Wye Valley. *'Union and Progress'* The Committee of Union and Progress, set up at Salonika by the Young Turks' revolution of 1908, deposed the Sultan Abdul-Hamid after forcing him to re-establish the constitution. Then, in the name of the Sultan's successor, Mohammed V, the committee ruled the Ottoman Empire.

51 *The Little Man,* a farcical morality in three scenes by John Galsworthy, was produced at the Birmingham Repertory Theatre on 15 March 1915. It was published in *The Little Man, and other satires* (Heinemann; Scribners, New York, 1915). *Rococo* A farce in one act by Harley Granville-Barker. It was produced at the Little Theatre, London, on 21 February 1911. It was published with *Vote by Ballot* and *Farewell to the Theatre* (Sidgwick & Jackson, 1917). *Pot of Broth* A play written by W. B. Yeats in association with Lady Gregory in 1902. It was produced at the Antient Concert Rooms in Dublin, 30 October 1902. It was published in *The Hour-Glass and other plays,* Plays for an Irish Theatre, vol. 2 (A. H. Bullen; Macmillan, New York, 1904). *12 pound look The*

Twelve-Pound Look by Sir James Barrie (1860–1937), a one-act comedy, was produced at the Duke of York's Theatre, 1 March 1910. It was published in *Half Hours: four one-act plays* (Hodder & Stoughton, 1914). *Feed the Brute* By Emily Morse Symonds (pseudonym George Paston) was produced at the Royalty Theatre, London, on 24 May 1908 (T. H. Lacy's Acting Editions, Samuel French, 1909). *Stanley Houghton* (William) Stanley Houghton (1881–1913), English playwright; his works included *Five One Act Plays: 'The Dear Departed', 'Fancy Free', 'The Master of the House', 'Phipps', 'The Fifth Commandment'* (Sidgwick & Jackson, 1913).

54 *Billy Sunday* William Ashley Sunday (1862–1935), American fundamentalist evangelist who from 1896 to 1935 conducted over three hundred religious revival meetings in major American cities. He reached the height of his fame in the New York City revival in 1917. *MacKail's Life* *The Life of William Morris* by John William Mackail (1859–1954) (Longmans Green, 1899).

56 *Spirit of Man* Robert Bridges' wartime anthology — see letter 40. I cannot find a quotation from this song in *The Spirit of Man*. *The Log of a Cowboy: a narrative of the old trail days* by Andy Adams (1859–1935) (Constable; Houghton Mifflin, 1903).

60 *Wootton* A small town near Oxford.

61 *the battle rages* The great German offensive from San Quentin began on 26 March 1918, and by the date of this letter it had penetrated the British line forty miles. The Germans succeeded in recapturing Bapaume, Péronne, and other towns they had lost in the Battle of the Somme.

63 *Webb* Captain Matthew Webb (1848–83), a native of Shropshire, completed the first successful crossing of the English Channel using the breast-stroke in August 1875. He died on 24 July 1883 in an attempt to swim the whirlpool rapids below Niagara Falls.

64 *when I was a boy* JM lived in New York City and Yonkers from March 1895 to July 1897 — see Introduction. *only laughter* During the battles of the Lys, 9–29 April 1918, the Germans opened up a wide breach in the British front, storming Messines Ridge and capturing Armentières.

67 *Boche drive* In the third Battle of the Aisne, 27 May–6 June 1918, the Germans attacked the French between Soissons and Rheims, capturing Soissons and reaching the Marne on 29 May. JM had visited most of the places mentioned in this letter during the preparation of his books on the Battle of the Somme.

68 *Gerard* James Watson Gerard (1867–1951), lawyer and diplomat. American ambassador to Germany, recalled in 1917; author of *My Four Years in Germany* (Hodder & Stoughton; Doran, 1917). The film, *My Four Years in Germany*, with Karl Dane, Ann Dearing, Willard Dashnell, directed by William Negh, was produced by Warner Brothers in 1918. *Prunella, or, Love in a Dutch Garden* Laurence Housman and Harley Granville-Barker (Sidgwick & Jackson, 1914). This play was first produced at the Court Theatre, London, on 23 February 1904. I have found no record of a film version. *a play with Mutt* The scene JM describes is in Charlie Chaplin's highly successful movie, *A Dog's Life* which was first shown on 14 April 1918. The dog is referred to as 'Mutt' but is in fact named Scraps.

72 *a marriage* On 3 July 1919 MB married Horace Joseph (1869–1943), senior philosophical tutor at New College, Oxford.

73 *lines of Browning* 'Bishop Blougram's Apology', 87–91.

Acknowledgements

Acknowledgements are due to the Society of Authors on behalf of the Masefield Estate for permission to publish John Masefield's letters and some of the poems; to Messrs Heinemann for other poems; to Lord Bridges for Margaret Bridges' letters; also to the *Southern Review*, in which Elizabeth Daryush's poem 'Armistice' first appeared.

The illustrations of Margaret and Edward Bridges are reproduced by kind permission of Lord Bridges; the frontispiece portrait of John Masefield was published in *Literary Digest*, 5 February 1916; the battlefield photographs were published in *Harper's Monthly Magazine*, May 1917.